Noel Bermondsey's number one Deejay

By Noel Smyth

Noel – Bermondsey's number one DJ

Dedication

To My Mum and Dad

Sisters Breda, Lill, Lorraine,

And my brother Pat.

Table of contents

Noel – Bermondsey's number one DJ

.

Introduction

BERMONDSEY BOUND

Drive over Tower bridge from east London, turn left into Tooley street and you have entered the utopia known as Bermondsey, a town full of duckers and divers, scallywags and vagabonds, people with good hearts, and a friendly nature. The flats of Devon Mansions end as Jamaica road begins, the iconic Holy trinity Dockhead church stands proud in red brick, at the edge of the manor, it will be the place I make my Holy Communion and confirmation, and later I was an altar boy there. Just round the corner was my two schools. Everything was so close together, I loved it then, like I love it today, I will always love Bermondsey.

My first impressions of Bermondsey as a young boy were of the friendly and generous dockers who worked on Chambers wharf. They would throw out fresh fruit to us kids waiting expectantly below the warehouse loop holes, oranges, lemons, and if you're lucky, some under ripe bananas, that had just arrived on cargo ships from the Caribbean. The fruit would rain down from the floors above. We would quickly collect as much as we could in our arms and then run off down Bevington street shouting "Mum, I got ya some bananas!" This is Bermondsey of the sixties, the land of plenty, even though we were all skint. Bermondsey people have big hearts. And in this memoir, you will see it, repeatedly

In 1969 I moved to Bermondsey from my first home 62 Campbell buildings near the Cut market in Waterloo. I was eight years old and was looking forward to my new challenges on the Dickens estate, a massive council estate that featured all the flats named after a character from those Charles Dickens classics "Oliver house" Pickwick house" and my block Rudge.

My new home was number 19 Rudge house on the fourth floor of five, four bedrooms and a splendid view of both sides of Jamaica Road and across the main junction that included the much-robbed Midland bank (now a posh apartment block), the Greg, and the shops under Spenlow house. Pete and Ada ran the sweet shop, and next door was a lady's hairdressers, where my mum got her hair done when we were going somewhere special.

Before our new home was decorated, I recall a rented twenty inch black and white tv from Rediffusion in the corner of the living room showing Neil Armstrong's first giant steps on the surface of the moon. I had just made mine in SE16.

It was quite early on and I was made aware of how the locals were so proud of everything Bermondsey, it was drilled into me by everyone I met. Local heroes like Tommy Steele Max Bygraves and the football legends of Millwall F.C, Harry Cripps Alan Dorney, and the brilliant Barry Kitchener. It wasn't long before my mum let me go to the Den with my new mates, Millwall played in all white then, and were in the first division, the Den had a vociferous atmosphere that intimidated the opposition before they ran onto the pitch, I loved the old Den. It didn't take long before I was falling in love with my new hometown and very soon, I too was boasting, if anyone asked where I was from? I would proudly reply "I'm from Bermondsey mate."

A few weeks later I was making new friends at my new school in George row, "St Joseph's" catholic school was just yards away from my flat on the Dickens estate, my secondary school was even closer "St Michael's," both schools run by the local Nun's from Dockhead convent which was next to our local church "Holy trinity Dockhead". My mum took a job as a dinner lady at St Josephs and when it came to dinner time at School, I'd never go hungry, she would pile the plate up with whatever was on offer. To be honest I think she was just keeping an eye on her son and filling his little tummy at the same time.

It was October and it was time for "Penny for the Guy", every year around this time we would make a "Guy" out of old clothes and rolled up newspapers. Firstly, stuff the paper into the old jeans and shirt and tie the ends up with string, place a deflated football on its shoulders and carefully attach a plastic Guy Fawkes mask with Sellotape to the ball. Wallop, you have made a Guy!

The best pitch was outside Ada and Pete's sweetshop in the row of shops under Spenlow house. The bus's stop right outside, on Jamaica road, so, first sign of a 70, 188, or 47 bus and us lads were on high alert. With great enthusiasm we would approach the people getting off the bus and politely ask "Penny for the Guy Mister?" or sometimes "Penny for the Guy Miss?" Some would ask to see the Guy first, before parting with a tanner, and others would say "I'll just get a paper and you can have the change". This was an easy way of raising funds for money to go towards buying Fireworks for the big night on November 5th. This was pre-decimalisation and people did give us old copper pennies, some with George V face on it. There were tanners and shillings, and if you were very lucky two bob. My favourite was a thrupenny bit, not just because it rhymed with tit, but it was a weird shape. There was a girl I fancied who collected them, she slapped me round the face when I asked if there was any chance of seeing her "Thrupenny bits?" I thought it was funny, she obviously didn't. We were only nine back then.

Once our collection tin started to fill up with coppers, we were tempted to pop into the sweetshop for some fruit salads or black jacks, we used to get eight for a penny then. Or a thru pence worth of cola cubes. Those were the days.

I had so much fun with my new mates from the estate. Albert Lawson, Gary Pritchard, Frankie Deegan, Tony Cornish, we played knock down ginger, run outs and epic games of football Tennis and cricket while waiting for Joe the ice cream man. When we heard his jingle, everything stopped. Hopefully, I could afford an oyster with a flake and strawberry juice if I was lucky. That was a special treat. I would call up "Mum, Joe's here" She would throw down the coins from our fourth floor flat in a tissue and float down a plastic Tupperware dish, Joe would fill the container up with ice cream with red juice poured over it and a couple of chocolate flakes. This would be for dessert, after our traditional Sunday roast chicken dinner.

We had the toffee apple man, the coalman, and visitors at the door including the gas man, the provident man not forgetting the man from Littlewoods pools. Lots of water has passed under Tower Bridge in the past fifty years, and this book will highlight how I got to this point in a colourful journey as Bermondsey's number one DJ, and eventually we will find out how Bermondsey radio got started and succeeded in helping our community in its hour of need. I hope you enjoy the read, and maybe one Sunday, tune in and find out what all the fuss is about, Bermondsey radio, listen once, and you will be hooked. That is a promise.

CHAPTER ONE

SAUCEPAN LIDS

Growing up on the Dickens estate was fantastic, us kids were out playing in the summer sunshine till gone 9pm or at least till we were called in by our parents. We would play great football matches on the grass in front of Rudge House and Cricket on Wrayburn's grass in front of the block, back to Rudge for tennis in the square with a wall as a net, nowadays it is the residents car park but back in the day it gave us hours of fun emulating our heroes on the centre court at Wimbledon.

Jimmy Connors, John McEnroe, Bjorn Borg, and the charismatic Ilie Nastase.

Times were so different then, I remember taking back empty bottles of lemonade and getting money for the empties and then knocking out the dosh on sherbet dabs, or maybe a Beano or a Dandy comic.

And another thing, the queue that would form on a Saturday at 5.30pm outside Pete and Ada's for the late edition of the Evening standard newspaper, with the up-to-date football results and league tables, gawd knows how they printed it so quickly. But they did.

I was quite a naughty young boy- a cheeky chappie, always trying to make people laugh, I was particularly good at it and on occasions got huge laughs even though I say so myself.

When I was ten, I went on my first school trip with St Josephs to Keswick in the Lake district, we stayed in a hostel just outside Keswick and I was sharing a room with a few of my buddies, we were in our room playing football with a tennis ball making one hell of a racket as you do. The room door flew open, and our teacher Miss Thompson shouted, "Smyth what do you think you're doing?"

"Nothing miss, honest" I replied, sounding a bit like Jack Wilde, (who played the artful dodger in the movie Oliver.) while flicking the ball under one of the beds hoping Miss Thompson would not see, but alas she did and asked me directly to retrieve the soon to be confiscated ball. I was standing their sweating uncontrollably in my pyjamas looking as guilty as O.J Simpson and she insisted "Get me that ball and get into bed and get some sleep we are off out on a coach trip in the morning" I got down on all fours and started to make my way under the double bed with my bum sticking up as I stretched for the elusive ball, Miss Thompson got down on all fours too and her nose was level with my buttocks when I let rip the longest fart of all time, within seconds the strong odour filled the room, it sounded like a tugboat going down the Thames, and smelt very eggy, and full of sulphate. I scrambled to my feet and handed the ball to Miss Thompson whose other hand was over her mouth, and she looked as though she was going to hurl "Get to bed you lot I'll see you all in the morning" The door slammed shut behind her and all of us in the room burst into fits of hysterical laughter. It was a great fart. It made a wonderful sound, and it didn't half pen and ink, I couldn't hold it in any longer I promise you. Anyhow it would have been a shame to waste it.

Later the next day I apologized to Ms Thompson for the previous night's embarrassing moment, and she was good about it, But I was in trouble again, soon after we made a souvenir stop in Keswick town centre. "Back on the coach in 30 minutes" Sister Delores had announced.

Half an hour later we were counted back on the coach and the driver set off back towards our hostel. Two of the Nuns came through the coach inspecting and commenting on our gifts for back home. "Oh Mary, that's a lovely tea towel you bought there, who's that for your mummy?" Mary nodded. As the Nuns got to where I was sitting their faces turned to thunder "Give me that please" Sister Clotilde insisted pointing at the paperback I had just bought in the souvenir shop she snatched it from my hands urgently and hid it from prying eyes and quickly shuffled to the front of the coach. (To read it later that evening I reckon)

It was the paperback of "Diamonds are forever" The Sean Connery film in the James Bond franchise, trouble was, the cover had a picture of "Bond" with two glamorous ladies either side of him with a lot of their boobies on show, I think the Nuns were protecting me as I was only ten, they never did return the book to me, but I had the last laugh, I watched the movie later that year on the tv.

I made it into the St Joseph's school nativity play, I was one of the three wise men, and I gave a gift to the new-born baby Jesus of frankincense, I do remember the play as a kid I had a wonderful blue turban and a one liner, if I could remember it. Sister Baptist was very pleased with my performance, she said I could be milk monitor for my class, promotion at last.

My mum worked at the school as a dinner lady and myself and Eddie Webber held the record for going up for apple crumble and custard sixteen times each, don't know where we put it, but my mum and the rest of the dinner ladies were laughing each time we went to the serving hatch. Dinner money for each day was twelve new pence, so we wanted to get our money's worth.

I do recall being in a dentist's chair at Guys hospital at the age of ten, having a check up on the 25th floor, rinsing my mouth out with that pink water, and spitting the gargled stuff into the tiny sink. My dentist then said something that has stayed with me all my life. "No fillings today, Noel, but if you don't look after your teeth, they will all fall out before you are 30!" Blimey, I better look after them then. My teeth as a youngster were never white, always a yellow colour, it was because of the drugs my mum was taking at the time whilst pregnant with me. I did take the dentist's advice, even though he used scare tactics. Basterd.

Growing up, I was never no trouble, even though, all around me kids on the estate were getting in trouble with the old bill. I was a well-behaved young man, and the friends in my circle were all far more interested in playing all the different sports available to us, and we were all lucky to steer clear of trouble with the police, us saucepan lids were sports mad. I must admit we did play knock down ginger, and that could annoy the residents a little.

I was so good; I became an altar boy at Dockhead church. This meant turning up at Church, getting dressed in the Altar boy vestments and assist the priest with Mass, this included ringing the bell at the appropriate time, for example, when the Priest broke the bread into the Chalice. Another thing was when holy communion was being given to the congregation the altar boy would hold a communion-plate under the chin of the recipient that is about to receive holy communion. There wasn't much to it, and I don't know what happened, but I didn't last very long as an altar boy. I do remember Michael Barrymore, who went to St Michaels, was one of the senior ones, and he went on to be the biggest star on British television.

At eleven years of age, I started at St Michael's school and went through in the same "A" class throughout my time at the school, I was allocated "Alban" house and a yellow tie, to signify my allegiance to the house. Alpha was top class with all the clever kids, then followed A (my class), B and C respectively. If you were in C class you had one sandwich short of a picnic, a bit dim some would say.

When I started Miss Burns was the Head Mistress and was soon replaced my sister Anne upon her retirement. We had a few nutty teachers at the time, Mr Murphy was sports and a very good teacher, Mr O'Brien was geography and very good. Miss Fletcher was completely mad, and her voice was something out of a horror movie.

During tea-breaks us lads would play penny up the wall, while someone would keep dog-eye for teachers. Every so often there would be a fight between students and after school we would follow the crowd to under Lupin point to cheer on the brawlers. Lupin point was a 20-floor block of flats on the junction of Jamaica road and abbey street. It would take place under ground in the lit car park, where the garages were. In my year Victor Charles was the best, a black muscular young man, but he always ended up fighting under Lupin point for one reason or another. He was a nice guy though.

I do remember having violin lessons behind the stage in the assembly hall for a couple of weeks, I have no idea why I stopped going, maybe I couldn't afford a violin of my own, or just couldn't play it.

At my careers interview I stated I wanted to be a DJ on the radio as my job of choice, but as a second choice I put BT Engineer, well it seems dreams do come true, my first choice came true even though I had to wait till March 2020, but I will get to Bermondsey radio in the second half of the book, I will get to it eventually I promise.

So, we were lining up outside the main hall at St Michael's for our B.C.G jab, this area was near to the headmaster and deputy head's offices, and we were told "No talking" so what do you think I was doing at this time? Yep, you got it, rabbiting away like it was going out of fashion. Suddenly there was a tap on my shoulder and my ear was grabbed and pulled high above where it should been, it was Mr Blake, otherwise known as Blakey, and I was marched on tip toes by the deputy head to his office, once inside he shut the door and let go of my throbbing ear and went behind his desk "Right Smyth, is it a week suspension? or three of the best? you choose".

I said "I'll have a week off please Sir"

I can't believe my reply, this did not go down too well with Mr Blake (Deputy head)

"I am just going to ring your mother and see what she has to say on the matter"

After a short word with my mum, he handed the phone to me and said "Smyth, your mother wants a word"

"Take three of the best and when you get home, I'll give you three of the best and a lot more besides" my mum insisted. Do not think she was too pleased either.

This is not going to plan.

"So, Sir I am going to take three of the best, I've changed my mind Sir" I said bravely.

He already had the cane in his hand, a four-foot thin piece of bamboo and was limbering up with a few practice swipes.

"Bend over Smyth" Blakey instructed me

Ten seconds later I was upright, and the pain hit me, I thought I was going to faint, that bloody hurt! I left Blakey's office bravely joining my mates in the que for my B.C.G I didn't say a word, that was the first and last time I had the cane during my time at St Michael's. I was a good boy really. I shouldn't have been talking, I guess.

It was about this time I started to get into music, I got a transistor radio the size of a packet of Benson & Hedges with a small speaker built-in plus headphones, every night in bed I would tune into radio Luxembourg for all the latest tunes and golden oldies with great DJ's, the radio was used a lot for football commentaries too. At this time, I was twelve years old and working as a paperboy for Len Burdett's newsagents/sweetshop near the old Dockhead stores pub and delivered the daily papers to flats on the Arnold, Kirby, Neckinger and Dickens estates. The Kirby estate later became famous for decorating the whole of the estate with England flags every time England's men or women took part in a football tournament, hundreds of flags would come out and be displayed all over the estate. I told you Bermondsey people were patriotic.

The few pounds I earned would go towards special stuff for me, a red Raleigh chopper bike was bought via the Freemans catalogue at

£1.50 a week and helped me deliver those papers so much quicker. A record player (with speakers) was the next purchase, and the best thing I treated myself to. This record player started me on my way to collecting vinyl records, the first record I bought was Bohemian Rhapsody by Queen, it was bought at the soapy jack's electrical store on Jamaica road, with the junction with Drummond Road. Very soon I was collecting records and it soon became my hobby and passion, and still is fifty years on, except these days in 2022 I purchase and download the songs off the internet and play them digitally at these modern-day gigs. Back in the early seventies I bought vinyl records by Slade, David Bowie, and Elton John, I used to love Slade. Noddy Holder, the lead singer, had a unique voice, bit like Miss Fletcher at St Michael's. I still play their Christmas number one to this day. Merry Christmas everybody, one of the best.

My brother Pat gave my mum a reel-to-reel recording machine for her birthday which was extremely high tech and of course I was the only one who could use it, my mum had not a scooby doo (Clue) what buttons to press, so I used it a lot. I hooked it up with our stereo and tuned it to Capital radio and sat there for hours recording tracks off the radio broadcast. As the DJ introduced the next song, I would release the pause button and record the song, towards the end, I would be poised to press the pause button to complete the recording. The art was to avoid any more words from the DJ, I became a master of this recording technique, and soon had all the chart songs recorded. Minus the DJ chatter. My favourite deejays at the time were Noel Edmunds, Kenny Everette, and loved listening to the new chart on a Tuesday afternoon on Radio one.

My sister Breda was having a party at her place in Woolwich and I brought the machine along and connected it to her stereo system and started to play some tunes, The Real thing, Shalamar, John Holt, everyone was dancing to the music, then one of my brothers mates Malcolm came up to me and asked "How much do you charge

Noel ?" he was serious, he wanted to book me for a party at a tenants hall at the end of the year ! I thought to myself for a moment and blurted "£30 till midnight"

Malcolm held out his hand and while shaking my hand he said, "done deal" and that was my first booking. But hold your horses, how the hell am I going to play at a proper party in a tenant's hall without the essential speakers, decks, and flashing lights?

This is where my mum came to the rescue, she worked very hard as a dinner lady at St Joseph's and when I went to St Michael's she got a job there too. She was brilliant, only thinking about her son and with the help of provident cheques we went down JW Parker down the Old Kent Road, and got twin decks, speakers and some lighting and I called my roadshow "Capricorn Disco" my DJ career was about to get underway. Thanks to my mum.

Malcolm cancelled my first gig due to a relative falling ill, so instead I was off to Wembley for a wedding reception party, it would be fun mixing all the party songs for the newlyweds. My brother was my roadie as I was vanless and with no driving license just yet. I was taking lessons and had my eye on a ford escort van that I saw down blue anchor lane in the old Ford dealership.

The playing of the records was the easy bit, using the microphone and announcing the first dance was the biggest challenge because of my shyness and nerves, I did not want to cock it up, and as it turned out there was no dramas, thank God.

The first time I used the mic to make an announcement informing the guests "the buffet was now open", my paranoia was heightened, and my nerves increased, but somehow, I got my words across, loudly and clearly. I was barely eighteen years of age and here I was starting on my DJ journey, who knows where it would take me, and how long it would last.

Later that year I passed my driving test on the third attempt, The crazy thing was, I stalled the car three times before I left the Hither green testing centre. I thought I failed so the rest of the test I relaxed and when I got back to the centre the examiner said "Well done Mr Smyth, you have passed" well, I couldn't believe it, my previous two tests were better than this one! I was over the moon and with the readies in my pocket I made my way down the blue to get my van. I wasted no time, when I got home, I phoned my insurance company and sorted things out with fords and half an hour later I had the Ford escort van keys in my hand.

I wish I had brought someone with me, up until this point I had never been in a vehicle on my own, I was behind the steering wheel of my rust bucket of a van, I checked it was in neutral before nervously turning the key in the ignition into first gear and away it went. I turned right into Southwark Park Road, and at the lights turned right into St James Road.

My next decision was a bad one, I turned right into blue anchor lane and drove back down towards the dealership where I had just bought the van. This lane had cars parked on both sides of the road and was barely room for two vehicles to pass each other traveling in opposite directions. Nobody told me!

Coming towards me in a brand-new Ford escort van with less than 10 miles on the clock, was a proud new owner who beckoned me through, I was going as slow as I could, but I heard metal on metal, I had a "collision" within five minutes of getting in my rust bucket.

Damage on the brand-new van was small and was repaired by rubbing t-cut on the scratch and the new owner was quite good about it. My van was fine although I told the van driver jokingly, to be more careful next time. He said, "He would" and did a noisy wheel spin and burnt some rubber as he sped off down Blue Anchor lane like James hunt.

My Dad died of a heart attack in 1979 he was just 54 and I was only 17 at the time and it affected me badly, he worked as a porter in Waterloo station and worked the night shift. He rode his bicycle to and from his workplace, and did his best for his family, it wasn't nice how I found out about his passing.

I was working in the Venus fish bar on Jamaica Road serving fish and chips, normally with Alex and Chris, this was my first job since leaving school, they were on a day off, so there brother Bill was sitting in for them, Bill had half of his index finger on his right hand missing, due to an accident while trying to cut fillets of cod, it made him look like a Greek Dave Allen. the phone went in the shop Bill answered it, he turned to me very coldly "Go home son, your dad has died" it was the way he said it, no care, no feeling. I was devastated, heartbroken, he could have let me down more gently.

My dad came from County Meath in Ireland and moved to London in 1958 with my mum and sisters Breda and Lill, three more children followed, Pat, me, and Lorraine, all born in London. My dad's passion was football. He would take me to see Manchester United whenever he could, mostly in London at stadiums like Highbury, White hart lane, Stamford bridge, and Selhurst park. Many times, we would travel to Old Trafford and Together we watched Bobby Charlton, Dennis Law, and Georgie Best in their prime, it wasn't a bad way to start following a football team.

I miss my dad so much, it was a big blow to lose him at such an early age, that's when I needed him the most, I hope he is looking down on me and is very proud of the life I have led.

I didn't realise it at the time, but my mum must have been devastated losing her husband, but she carried on, and just a few months later, gave me an 18th birthday party at Wade Hall on the Dickens estate. How she organised this party I have no idea. She was grieving for my dad, but still wanted the best for me. Even though loads of friends and relatives turned up and we all had a great time, I was so very grateful for what my mum had done. But somehow It felt empty Wade Hall, without my dad.

My mum gave me a gold ring with ten chip diamonds in it, for my birthday. It was made by Mo Stevens, the local jeweller. And I have never taken it off in all these years. Today it's on my small finger on my right hand. It still shines bright and sparkles in the right light. It reminds me always of my parents, who encouraged me always to do my best.

CHAPTER TWO

LILLIPUT HALL (The Lill)

Simply the best, this pub was my local in old Jamaica road, on the junction with Abbey Street, owned by Billy Aird and his lovely wife Angie, God rest her soul. It was run by their mate from Liverpool Alan Price, who was a complete nutcase, he was a lovely man, but there was something weird about him peering through those thick rimmed glasses he wore, while smiling and asking you "How's the Crac mate?" in his broad scouse accent. I could tell you a tale or two about him, and I will tell you at least one before this chapter is complete.

"The Lill" was frequented by me and my mates every weekend, it was a music venue with a DJ booth in the centre of the pub against the wall and the dance floor was on its right, with the ladies and men's toilets either side of it, round the other side was a pool bar and the main bar was in a horseshoe shape. It had a Tetris video machine just inside the door, with a cigarette machine next to it. Benson and Hedges, Silk Cut, and Marlboro light. Further around there was a fruit machine and near the pool table was a phone box, that was fed by ten pence pieces. No mobile phones at this time, so the phone box was used to order cabs home, with the help of Dockhead cars.

It had an 11 o'clock license in those days, and it closed at 3pm in the afternoons opening for the evening session at 7pm, Sunday had a noon start with last orders at 3pm. If you fancied it, you could have a late one. The "Lill" was one of the first pubs in southeast London to get an extension to midnight. It would later get a 2am license and was one of the busiest pubs in South-east London.

Fridays in the early eighties we would all meet at the boatman, otherwise known as the "Royal George" on Jamaica road at around 7pm, we had a Ching (a fiver) whip, my drinking buddies consisted of my best mate Albert Lawson, John Sullivan, Colin Foot, Steven Clarke, and anyone else who cared to join us. My fashion sense was a bit weird to say the least. On one occasion I walked down Jamaica road in pvc trousers and a Spandau Ballet top, I looked a right prick. When I got down the Vic in pages walk, we were joined by my mate Colin Foot, he took one look at me and burst into fits of laughter, pointing at my pvc strides he said "Smudge, you look a right donut!" Cheers mate, I thought. And needless to say, I never wore those trousers again. Despite this harsh criticism it was great to see everyone each week and chat about the latest episodes of "Only fools and horses" and all the other great shows on the tv, but really the mission every Friday night was easy, to get rotten drunk, spangled, legs akimbo in other words get pissed!

The pub crawl had begun, and next stop was "The Lill" just for a couple of lagers, then down "The Fellmongers" for the old dance tunes, it was always a lively boozer, and was run by Bobby Crawford, And if you asked me what song I associate with "The Fell" it would be "going underground" by The Jam, I know this is not a dance tune, but all the chaps would love to sing-along to it. After a few sherbets we would cross into Pages walk to the "Queen Vic". This pub I worked in for a while and really enjoyed it. We would spend a good hour listening to the indie chart sounds before strolling back to the "Lill" via the usual route, Grange Road, and Spa Road for the final knockings. We would all stagger home noisily along old Jamaica road, throwing orange parking cones at each other. Every Friday night Steven Clarke would attempt to leapfrog a royal mail post box, I think he would often get stuck on the top, and we would have to help him down. The post box is still there next to St James school and Bowley house. We were drunk as skunks, we were pissed, it was mission accomplished.

Drinks at the "Lill" on a Monday night with my mate Albert was legendary, we would meet up at 8pm and get sloshed, Chinese on the way home at Silver Sea Dockhead (before they moved the take-away next to the Fleece in Abbey Street). My order would be something like this …Piece of chicken chow mein, pancake roll, chips, and curry sauce, it never got eaten, I would find it Tuesday morning, hardly touched, on the living room floor, then I would bin it, and set off, late, to work. Even so, it was bought every Monday night religiously.

One Monday night myself and Albert met up as usual and for some reason the drinks were coming thick and fast and by 10pm we were rotten, we were joined by Billy Aird, the guvnor of the pub, and for those that don't know, Billy was a professional heavyweight boxer who had recently fought for the British heavyweight title and lost to John L Gardner, due to the fact he had too many things going on his life including the purchase of the pub. More drinks followed and I started to slow down considerably and wobble a bit, the pub started to spin and wallop! I vomited over Billy's lap! "Fuckin hell Noel I just had these dry-cleaned" referring to his trousers. He stormed past me, I thought I was going to get a right hander, instead he went upstairs changed and came back and continued drinking with us, as though nothing had happened. This shows you the humility of the man, I can say he was the best guvnor I ever worked for, and I will be forever grateful for the opportunities and work he gave me.

A Sunday drinking session in the pub round by the pool bar and the conversation turned to deejays in the pub. Billy asked if I would be interested in doing the prime Friday night slot, he was not too pleased with the guy who was currently doing it. I jumped at Billy's offer and came out with a line my friends continually give me grief to this day "I'll put the "Lill" back on the map Bill" It was a boastful prediction, said in jest, we all laughed, including Billy, and they all took the piss out of my bold promise. And the rest is part of Bermondsey folklore.

The pub had gorgeous barmaids, Joyce was there serving behind the bar on that infamous Monday night, Rita, and her bespeckled side kick Chris were a great laugh, there was the beautiful Janice, and Chris and Fred were great company too. I remember Billy would get me to announce engagements of his barmaids, if they were ever caught fraternising with any of the male customers, Billy liked to embarrass them, it would make him laugh, but make his barmaids blush.

Deejaying in the "Lill" was something I always looked forward to, every Friday night was party night and in the early eighties, they had their own DJ booth with twin turntables and space inside to bring in your own boxed collection, including 7" and 12" inch singles and albums, there was a microphone for announcements, the door of the booth was left open for punters wanting a request or dedication on the mic. Connected to the PA was 6 Bose speakers dotted round the pub and the sound was loud but clear. I do miss playing vinyl records, always make sure you play the right side, and not the B side. This could be an instrumental version of the A side and be very embarrassing if you lost concentration and played it by mistake.

We formed a pool team at the Lill and competed with other local pub teams on a Tuesday night, singles and doubles matches and I was the captain, not that I was the best player, just Billy chose me, and that was that. We did ok, it was a good laugh, and a great way to socialise on a

Tuesday night. What I remember the most was that at some point during the match, plates of food would come out from the team that was hosting. Loads of it, sandwiches, sausages, chicken legs it was unbelievable.

One night it all kicked off in the pub round my side near the dance floor it involved about six lads, and drinks were going up in the air and fists were flying, my job was to turn the music off and wait for Billy or the bouncers to sort it out. One of our wonderful barmaids Rita was out near me collecting empty glasses and she looked worried as she made her way towards the DJ booth, she jumped in the booth as glasses and bottles were being thrown in all directions, before I had time to greet her a bloke pulled her out of the box, and he jumped in and shut the door behind him, thinking he was safe. This lump of a guy was now standing next to me, I could not believe a bloke would do this to a young lady. Billy was soon on the scene and the troublemakers ejected, including the guy who sheltered in my DJ booth. Rita was laughing about it later when we were having a staff drink. It just shows you what people will do. I continued to play the party music again and the pub continued undeterred till closing.

I was walking down Jamaica road after midnight towards the "Lill" I just finished a gig locally and the "Lill" had a 2am licence for this special fancy dress party so I was gagging for a pint, and I knew all my mates were dressed up in costumes and waiting for me to join them.

I was making slow progress, I was dressed as Papa Smurf, a costume I borrowed from my workplace, it was an authentic costume that was used by the "National" petrol garages for their promotions. Even though it was 12.30am I was getting noticed by car and van drivers that were bibbing there Hooter's at me. The costume was heavy and all in one up to the neck with a zip up the back, my mum had helped zip me up before I left Rudge house. It had a white beard that attached to my ears and a massive blue hat that tied under my chin. When I entered the pub, my mates were all laughing at my ridiculous costume, I was grasping £100 in my furry hand and asked Darren if he would look after it as I had no pockets, he took the money. This was a bad move. The place was rocking, I ordered a pint of lager and the sound of Motown classics, Lou Rawls, Teddy Pendergrass filled the pub, there was nothing like a great night in the "Lill." Now the ladies turned their attention to my tail, they loved my tail, playing with it suggestively and one even tried to mount it!!

Meanwhile I was trying to find Darren who had taken care of my ton, it soon became clear he had gone home with my £100.

One Saturday around 11pm I arrived in the pub a little worse for ware, on my own, and went round to have a drink round the other side by the pool table, this was a quiet part of the pub although the place was packed on this night. I was now sitting at the bar watching the games of pool taking place in front of me. An elderly gentleman joined us and got Alan Price's attention "Pint of Fosters please" he requested. Alan turned got the glass and started to pour the man's drink in a rounded glass, it was filled and placed in front of the gentleman. "I wanted a straight glass" he said sternly "Sorry mate we're busy tonight and run out of straight glasses" Alan retorted in his scouse accent. He took the gentleman's money and thought nothing more.

The elderly gentleman took the pint of Fosters in the bowl glass and downed it in one, he turned and went to the men's toilets with his emptied bowl glass in hand. A couple of minutes later he returned to the bar briefly and placed the bowl glass upon it with a steaming piece of his own excrement in the centre of the glass, he made haste, and had it on his toes. By the time Alan had noticed the soiled bowl glass on the bar and disposed of it discreetly and professionally the elderly gentleman was miles down the frog and toad.

A few years later Alan Price had a word with me, Billy had said that I should leave the "Lill" and help my friend Albert Lawson in his new pub the "Swan & Sugarloaf" just across the road in Dockhead. This was a truly kind gesture to Albert and his new venture. It once again shows how kind and generous Billy could be.

The Swan & Sugarloaf was a nice modern pub with a fantastic sound system, Bose speakers on all four corners. the bar was made of smart brickwork, and it already had a reputation for great soul music, the tv series "London's Burning" was filmed in there, for the pub scenes, and across the road the Dockhead fire station was used for its work scenes.

Albert had big plans for the pub and one Monday night he booked Radio London's Steve Walsh to pull in the crowds. Steve was very famous on the club scene and had a massive hit record with a re-working of the Fatback anthem "I found Lovin" on Steve's version you could hear his dulcet tones shouting, "You what, you what, you what" anyway, only a dozen people turned up and Bobby Crawford (The Manager) told him in no uncertain terms to "Fuck off" and he wasn't getting paid. It was a shame as Steve was a nice person and a fantastic DJ, but he left empty handed and slightly embarrassed about the situation.

Many great nights in the Sugarloaf, people would travel from all over southeast London for Saturday soul night, music from Maze, Al Green, Johnny Bristol, I loved playing music there, always a great atmosphere.

In the early days of Alberts ownership of the pub, Johnny Spring, the owner of Dockhead cars popped in for a drink or two, it was such a great night, Johnny took the mic from me and started effing and blinding, singing, and joking it was so funny I was crying with laughter and so was most of the others in there that night.

The next day we heard the sad news that Johnny had passed away, Gladys his wife was devastated and the following weekend I had a small gift for her, it was a recording on a cassette tape of Johnny entertaining us that night. All the singing, the swearing, the joking, she loved it, and said to me "Noel, that is so kind of you, I will treasure this, and will listen to it when I need cheering up, thank you so much"

"Your welcome Gladys, Your Welcome" I said emotionally.

My first concert I went to was Squeeze at the Hammersmith Odeon, great venue, and what a great first gig to go to. Little did I know I would meet all the members of the band except for Jools Holland at the Bermondsey carnival. I went with John Sullivan & Steven Clarke, and it was a fantastic gig. They played all the hits "Cool for cats" "Up the junction" it was a great introduction to live music.

The Pub game these days has changed quiet a lot, The opening times for one. In the good old days, we would have "Late ones" which meant you could buy more drinks after the final bell had been rung. The final bell notified drinkers that the pub was about to close, or not, if you were lucky to get a late one.

Nowadays pubs can stay open all day, and most do. In 2007 a new law came in banning smoking in pubs, smokers were banished outside in the pouring rain to satisfy their habit. For all you youngsters that haven't experienced a pub pre-2007 you would be shocked at the shear density of the smoke that enveloped the place. Dotted round the bars and tables were dozens of ashtrays, covered in advertising, and full of cigarette butts. Not a great odour, didn't look great either. Lots of Bermondsey's thriving boozers ended up closing, to be replaced by flats or Mosques, it's a shame but it's the sign of the times. The Lill, Samsons, Gilly's, all very busy pubs in there day, all gone. And they won't be coming back.

15th July 1981 I went on my first ever holiday to Crete in the Greek islands, on an 18-30 package holiday with my mates John Sullivan, Richie Adams, and Paul Gosling. It was my first time on an airplane, and I was pooping my pants as we took off. Four and a half hours later we landed on Greek soil, and we quickly scampered off to find our cases going around on the airport baggage carousel. Once collected we all went through customs control and boarded our 18-30 coach back to Hersonissos and our 4-star hotel. The heat was unreal on the way back to the hotel, boiling hot, and we met our beautiful host Ruth, who would be introducing us to all the best bits of Crete. I fell in love with Ruth straight away, great tan, shiny white smile and massive Babylon's in a skimpy teal bikini. 38dd's would be about right. Forty years on I don't know how I remembered the Teal bikini. The next fourteen days I would be drooling over Ruth. Realistically she was way out of my league, but I could dream, couldn't I?

My first big mistake happened on the first full day. The Hotel had a large swimming pool and me and the boys spent our time drinking and lounging around the pool all day. We had around twenty females in our company, all under thirty, and all topless!! I didn't know where to put my eyes. It was a strange experience, but I think we all got used to it by the final day. The big mistake that I had made was I hadn't applied any suncream throughout our first full day in the sun. When I got back to the room, I hastily tried to soothe the skin with some after sun, it was too late. I was on fire; my skin was burning while I was still wearing it. The faces of my room mates told the story as they would wince as I tried to administer more cream. I was in big trouble. Very soon I had two very large blisters forming where my polo shirts sleeve would cover on my arm. They looked like a water filled condom on each arm, stretching from the shoulder to the elbow joint. Even taking a cold shower was painful, any small amount of heat would be unbearable. Later trying to get my jeans on took me forever. But nothing was going to stop me going out on my first night in Crete. I was drinking large scotches in our room and took some pain killers, and it did help to ease the pain a little bit. So, we were out!

We went for a pizza down the road and the pain was becoming bearable, but I wasn't very comfortable, to say the least. What do you think happened on our first night in Crete? We only went and pulled didn't we. My one, (a German girl) must have loved my red lobster face and blue eyes, she was as drunk as me and all of us went back to our hotel, we were all staying at the same hotel. After more drinks on the sofas in the hotel lounge, I was getting a little friendly with Helga, and put my left arm around her shoulder, my arms were still inflated with blisters on them both. Out of nowhere I cracked a very funny joke and Helga laughed so much she rolled forward and then smashed her head back onto my blister which popped and covered her golden locks with its contents. I yelled out in pain; they could hear my screams in Corfu. I got a tissue and tried to wipe the puss out of her hair, she was very apologetic in a very drunken way. My mates were rolling about laughing their heads off, got no sympathy from them. Helga got up and said goodnight, I stood up and said I would escort her to her room. After painfully climbing the stairs leading to her room, when we got there, I thought, with a little luck, I was going to get me leg over here, instead, I got a peck on the cheek, and she wished me goodnight. I got to the top of the stairs leading back to my mates in the room below. Johnny Sullivan asked me "How did you get on?" When I reached the bottom step, I just turned to them all and shaking my head said, "Fucking Germans" The whole place erupted with laughter, even I joined the laughter, I was in pain, but even I, was finding it very amusing.

The next morning, I was hanging and very sore, all over. I wasn't going nowhere near any sunlight for a day or two, I thought. I thought wrong.

I stayed in my room in the shade trying to keep cool, I felt like Dracula must have felt when sunlight shone on his skin. I was planning on leaving my coffin, I mean room. That very evening for a Greek meal in the centre of town. Later on, that night I had a cold shower and sat on the edge of my bed looking at my wranglers, it was mind over matter I must get them on somehow. It took me at least half an hour to pull them on, over my burnt skin on my thighs. Watching me walk down the sandy lanes down towards town, must have looked like watching John Wayne on hemeroids.

Who do you think we bumped into while we were eating our Greek meal? Yes, it was Helga, she was all over me like a rash, if you'll pardon the pun. I was trying to eat my calamari, and she kept putting her tongue down my ear hole. I got the message, and after finishing my moussaka, we were hand in hand walking down to the very windy beach. The waves were crashing onto the golden sand. I looked around and Helga was practically naked just her thong was still in place. Bloody hell. What is going on here? Suddenly, I have turned into David Hasselhoff, never had this luck with the girls back home. I was wearing Obsession by Calvin Klein, do you think me after shave had something to do with all this? Helga, meanwhile, was writhing around on the sand stark bollock naked, her private parts were winking at me. I was in big trouble; my Wranglers were stuck to my blistered skin. I couldn't get them off. I was gutted. Helga was livid, she got dressed and walked off up the beach on her Jack Jones. I was now trying to get my jeans back on, took me an hour. When I got back to the hotel my pals were having drinks on the same sofas as the night before, in the hotel lounge. "How did you get on Smudge?" Richie asked. "I couldn't get my jeans off" I repeated, "I couldn't get my jeans off" once again the whole lounge was crying with laughter, at my expense. It wouldn't be the last time they would all laugh at my bad luck.

Helga left the next day, back to Germany, she didn't say goodbye, Life goes on. In a few days my skin healed, but I stayed out of the sun for the rest of my holiday, my skin has never recovered to this day. A few days later we all went and had a go at water skiing at the pier at the end of the beach. I was the last to go, Richie, John, and Gosey all had a wonderful time, had a long ride on the skis around the bay. It was now my go. Spiro the instructor, told me the rules, legs slightly bent, arms straight in front of you, but don't pull on the rope. Within ten minutes, Spiro wanted to kill me, he called me malaka!! (Greek for wanker) A hundred times. I broke his rope. My skis flew off and were fifty metres apart, the speed boat had to retrieve them for me. I had about eight attempts at it, and on the last go I was going through the water headfirst hanging on to the rope like superman. The instructor Spiro gave up on me and told me to swim back to shore. Good job I was wearing my buoyancy jacket, I made my way back to the pier after about half an hour, and asked Spiro if I could have another go, he told me to "Go away" in Greek. I was only joking with him; I don't want to see another pair of skis as long as I live.

What could possibly go wrong on this holiday now, I still have a week to go. But it does get a lot worse.

A couple of days later we were on the beach knocking back the beers, I was under a sun umbrella and laying back on my sun lounger hiding from the sun. It was bloody hot, about 95 Fahrenheit and rising. Richie said he was going for a swim, I jumped up from my sun lounger and decided to join him. We had boiling hot sand underfoot as we stepped gingerly towards the clear waters of the Mediterranean. When the sea was up to my waist, I could see how clear the water was. I could see my toes, and swimming round my legs were a shoal of dark coloured fish, each the size of a fishfinger and twenty or so in the group, they were following their leader out to sea, and Richie and I was about to do the same. After a few breast strokes, I could no longer touch the ocean floor and was treading water. Half a minute later and it was very deep, and the waves were getting a bit choppy. I suddenly realised I was going out to sea without even trying. My head was getting covered by the swell of the sea and for the first time I thought I was in trouble. I was treading water but seemed to be getting dragged out even further. I called out to Richie and told him I was, if you pardon the expression, out of my depth. I needed to get back to the safety of the dry land. He agreed it was getting dangerous, he was a very good swimmer, unlike me, I have no doubt, that if Richie was not there, I was a gonna. He helped me back. In fact, I think he saved my life. The biggest relief was when my toes could touch the sea floor again, I felt in control again, and exhausted and shaken up a bit, I slumped back into my sun lounger knowing I just had a close shave with death. I got totally pissed that night, for a change.

Our Holiday was up in Crete, so many life experiences, two weeks I will never forget for various reasons. We staggered up the stairs and took up our seats at the very front of the aircraft. All four of us were rotten drunk and could be heard the full length of the Boeing 737 aircraft singing "Lady Di, Lady Di, Lady Di" It was the 29th of July 1981, we were flying back to England the day Prince Charles married Lady Diana Spencer. The air stewardess came up to us and said if we didn't stop singing, she would have us ejected from the aircraft. Well, we shut up immediately, fastened our seat belts and not long after take-off we were all fast asleep. We arrived back at Gatwick my three amigos had wonderful tans, I looked white as a sheet, my lobster look had disappeared during the flight back home, and the skin on my nose was peeling. What a first holiday in the sun that was.

Chapter 3

Radio Guy's (Guys Hospital Radio)

Voluntary work at Radio Guys was something I really enjoyed doing from the early eighties, learning to present Radio shows was the next step in perfecting my deejaying and I looked forward to my visits to the super professional Radio Guys studios, which could be found on the first floor above WH Smith's, opposite Guys Tower. I would attend Monday and Thursday evenings from around 5pm till 10pm, and us budding deejays would each receive a 65p food voucher for our voluntary service, to be used in the staff canteen in the basement of the nurse's quarters near Hunts house. In those days we played vinyl records, and they were stored in shelves in the main room, but I liked to bring my own records in to play on my show, it was an easier process. There was Teac reel-reel tape machines to play custom made jingles, these machines not too different to the one my brother bought my mum, and I utilised. Then there were cart machines to play the stations ids. These cart machines would play the professionally made jingles with great sound, clarity, and timed precision. When I wasn't presenting a show, I could be engineering/producing a colleagues show, and in-between times helping others with various audio tasks, like making a jingle or a special mix for a show that could be used later. It wasn't the case of turning up and going straight on air presenting your own radio show. The management of Radio Guys would check you out first, including your temperament. You had to have several weeks of training, learn how to manipulate the buttons and faders and had to do your fair share of collecting requests from the wards. Then, you might have a chance of a practise show. It was a great way of weeding out the time wasters and super stars.

Going round the wards and collecting requests was how you got listeners and the maternity wards were favoured as the patients were in a good mood. "Isn't she lovely" by Stevie Wonder was a good song for a new-born baby girl, and "Beautiful boy" by John Lennon was a good one for a boy, although it could vary a lot. I lost count of the times I would encounter breast feeding, maybe this was the reason visiting the maternity wards was a popular choice, but it was all part of the job, and my blushes were spared by a deliberate cough or two as I entered these delicate areas.

While collecting requests one day in another part of the hospital with my clipboard and pen at the ready I walked up to a middle-aged man, who was sitting upright, I introduced myself "Hi my name is Noel from Radio Guys can I play you a song tonight in my request show at 7pm?" as I got closer I noticed a hole in his windpipe, oh shit I thought, the man tried to speak and instead vomit erupted from the hole in his throat, I apologised and called a nurse to help him , that will teach me not to dive in without first checking the condition of the patient, thankfully the nurse made the gentleman comfortable and I turned and approached the next bed across from him a lot more cautiously. This gentleman was not in bed but sitting in a chair next to it reading a book and as I approached, he peered over his reading glasses and before I had a chance to say anything he said, "Do you have any Peter Skellern?" "Yes, I believe we do, putting on the ritz, for sure" he put his thumb up in my direction and said, "That will do nicely, what time shall I tune in?" then suddenly I recognised who I was talking to, it was Richard Stilgoe, a tv presenter on the BBC program Nationwide, that also was presented by Frank Bough, he also worked on Esther Rantzen's That's Life! And collaborated with none other than Sir Andrew Lloyd-Webber on some of his West end musicals. "I shall play it just after 7pm sir" I said, he thanked me and assured me he would tune in, I wished him well and set off to the studio to plan my special celebrity request show.

Radio Guys was available via a handset at the side of each hospital bed, channel one was our channel, and you could listen via a set of headphones, we broadcasted Monday till Thursday 6pm till 10pm with a variety of different music genres, pop, country, rock, reggae, disco, and the popular Radio Guys chart show. My show was called "Nurses choice", this is a show I invented myself, I would venture up to a random hospital ward and ask the staff nurse politely if any of her nurses would like to be on Radio Guys and have her top three songs played, a short interview in the studio with yours truly, I would play the third song for all the patients on the nurses ward, second choice for all the staff on her ward, and the number one song for anyone special in her life. This show got everyone involved on the ward, and they all tuned in to listen to the show, so it proved very popular. The nurses were very difficult to persuade to do the show, but once they committed, they loved it and I didn't mind it myself, someone had to do it. It was tough work interviewing nurses in their uniform.

One of my proudest moments while working at the station was when I arranged for Danny Baker to come in for an interview live on air, this was round about the time when Danny was presenting topical news items on the Six O'clock show with Michael Aspel and Fred Housego. I knew Danny from the Lilliput Hall pub where he used to drink occasionally, I had a chat with him, and we set up the interview.

Thursday night and at 7pm he called Radio Guys and let us know he was in the foyer of Guys tower, I went over to meet him and escorted him over the road and up to the studios, he went straight into the show with one of our top presenters, Mike Smith, and I have to say it was a great listen, very funny and entertaining. He stayed longer than we anticipated and afterwards told me how much he enjoyed it. Even to this day when I see any of his friends, I always tell them to mention me to him and say that I gave him his big break in radio, it always makes them laugh.

I cannot stress how important Radio guys was to my life and deejay career, the help I received from people like Alan Pleasants, Mike Smith, Barry Robbins, Ross Patterson, and Paula Kerr, was incredible, they welcomed me into the world of hospital radio with open arms, they taught me to present a radio program very professionally using jingles, mixes, and edits. My good friend from Bermondsey Paul Scales also gave Radio Guys a go as a presenter and did a bloody good job at it. one of the nicest guys you'll ever wish to meet and is a good friend of mine to this day.

My voluntary work at Radio Guys was something I enjoyed a great deal, when I started Bermondsey radio, my very own radio station, I used much of what I had learned at the station many years before, to present radio shows in a professional way each Sunday morning, to hopefully give you a show worth listening to. One of Radio Guys presenters and great bloke Danny Pietroni worked with me at the station and at the Swan & sugarloaf pub in Bermondsey, he has presented shows for Magic radio and is presently working for Smooth radio at the weekends. I would ring him occasionally in the coming years and ask a favour, "would you be so kind and mention the Bermondsey carnival on your wonderful Magic radio show?" and without hesitation he would plug the Bermondsey carnival for me each time I asked.

While working at Guy's I made some calls to BBC Radio one and they invited me to the studios for the day, this was a big day for me. Meeting Simon Bates, who had arranged my visit. And all the other radio one presenters. I arrived at 8am and stayed throughout the day, watching from behind the glass in the company of the engineer of each show. Simon Bates was a bit aloof; Andy Peebles was a lot friendlier, and it was interesting watching the way they connected with the outside broadcast for the radio one roadshow with Mike Read and Smiley Miley. They were set up at a beach in Wales somewhere. The highlight for me was being introduced live on the Steve Wright in the afternoon show. Steve was fantastic, he of course came from New Cross himself and spoke to me about presenting shows at his local hospital. Without warning he suddenly turned his attention to me sitting outside the studio, watching him through the glass, this is what he said to the millions of listeners, I was stunned and frozen and in disbelief as he announced, "We have a special visitor to radio one today, from Bermondsey, and a radio presenter at Guys Hospital radio, here in London, its none other than Noel Smyth!" Wow, I was gobsmacked, I didn't expect this at all. He then said "Noel, come on in and say hello to everyone!" Oh my god, as I rose from my chair and thumbled for the handle of the first of two doors to enter the studio. "Come on Noel, everyone is waiting for you" I opened the second door and was now in the live studio. Steve said, "What do you want to say to our millions of listeners?" I was quiet a distance from the live mic so hurriedly I shouted, "Hello mum!" Steve laughed, and jokingly said "Get Out!!" which I did closing the two doors behind me. Embarrassed I sat back alongside the engineer, Steve introduced the next song and took his headphones off came out of the studio, smiling at me he shook my hand and said "That was brilliant, you didn't take yourself too seriously and entered into the feeling of the show, that was great" he said with sincerity. I thanked him for my moment of stardom and couldn't wait to see if anyone had heard me. Quite a few had and loved it.

On the way home from Radio Guys, I would often go and see my good friend Kevin Girling, the owner of the Clarence Pub and one of the nicest fellas you will ever meet. Just a short walk from Guys hospital, it was situated on the corner of Battle bridge lane and Tooley street, the pub is no longer there, instead More London with Marks and Spencer food hall plus the Hilton Hotel reside where the Clarence once stood. These drinks after my show at Guys ended up with Kevin playing the recording of the show via the cassette machine in the pub, listening, and giving me advice on how I could improve my deejaying techniques. These drinks and banter were the funniest nights, so many times we would end up laughing with tears rolling down our cheeks and begging each other to stop repeating the punch line. We had some great laughs in that pub, I'll never forget those days, they were brilliant.

Bermondsey radio insight   over 300 people have downloaded the free Bermondsey radio android app in the play store.

CHAPTER 4

LIFE ON THE OCEAN WAVES- MV LA PALMA

The "Record Mirror" was my magazine of choice, informing me of the latest single releases and album reviews. It had a large weekly readership and I decided to put a small advert in it, and it proved to change my life forever, the advert went something like this…. Capricorn Disco available for weddings, birthdays, or any special occasion Tel ….

This small ad cost me thirty bob and got me a dream job on board a luxury cruise ship starting April 1986 and ending October 1990.

Arthur Belmont rang me after he saw my advert February 1986 and asked me if I was interested in a six-month contract on board the MV La Palma cruising the Mediterranean, Arthur was the agent and was booking the acts for that coming season. I said "yes" and went along to his house in Hounslow for an audition.

I brought with me a cassette of a radio show I had been presenting at Guys hospital on "Radio Guys" The show was called "Nurse's choice."

I arrived at his posh house in Hounslow and Arthur opened the door, looking a bit like Captain birds-eye, he had a bushy "uncle albert" type beard, he welcomed me in and told me he had another dozen DJs to audition that day. The house had a very nautical theme with framed pictures of cruise ships adorning the walls of his study. After a bit of small talk, he told me the entertainment team needed a Stage manager/DJ for the coming season. I told him of my DJ experience and presenting radio shows on hospital radio, I then passed him the cassette. He placed it into the machine turned the volume up and listened to the edited show, after about a minute he stopped the playback and looked at me and said "Noel, you sound very good on the radio, If you are available from April I would be prepared to offer you the six month contract £150 per week paid in Greek Drachma" He then gave me a copy of the contract and said "read it and if you like what you read, sign it at the weekend and post it back to me and I will see you at Heathrow. We will fly out at the end of April with the rest of the entertainment team to join the MV La Palma in Piraeus.

There and then I decided I was going to give it a go, I shook Arthur's hand and said I would read the contract and have it back to him by Saturday and look forward to working for him this coming season. I left his house on a high, the boy from Bermondsey done good. I ended up at Chariots, a smart pub opposite the old Peak Freans building. I couldn't wait to tell someone. It would turnout that I would work on the cruise ship till October 1990, April was the start of 5 fantastic years of life on the ocean waves.

When I first got the call from Arthur, I thought it was a wind up, I went along with it, and it paid off. Sometimes things happen and change your life path. It was as though doors were opening for me.

Preparations began with cashing in my insurance policy I was paying into, I went out and bought a whole new wardrobe of clothes, formal wear for the captain's cocktail parties, including dickie bows and wing collared shirts. I got a dinner jacket and a blue blazer from Next and some white flannel trousers and loads of polo shirts from the Freemans catalogue. New underwear, shorts, all the clothes had summer and the hot Mediterranean sun in mind. I had a special flight case made to transport my vinyl records and audio equipment, plus, some lighting. If you're going to do something, do it right.

The MV La Palma was 12,500 tonnes, holding 650 passengers, it was registered in Limassol Cyprus and owned by Intercruise Ltd. It was twice the length and twice as wide as the HMS Belfast, docked near London bridge, but weighed the same. Intercruise Ltd were based in Piraeus and had only one ship in their organisation. La Palma was equipped with a small swimming pool, a German beer garden, a nudist deck, Casino, boutique, hairdressers, hospital, restaurant, theatre lounge and nightclub/cinema. I loved the German beer garden, situated near the nudist deck. it was very popular with the German passengers. The beer was imported from the Spaten brewery in Munich, and it took a good five minutes to pour a glass of Spaten, due to the excessive froth on the top of the beer, the froth had to be got rid of, and topped up, that's why it took a while to pour. Once finished it really was a great tasting beer. To accompany a German beer would be sausages and a bread roll, with mustard or sour croute, this is a German tradition.

The crew onboard were mainly Greek, including the captain, his officers, and all the waiters and bar managers. Sadly, La Palma was broken up for scrap after the Athens Olympic games, where it was used as a floating hotel.

My inside cabin onboard was small, had two beds a large wardrobe shower/bathroom and was situated next to the restaurant, because I worked late in the nightclub I was allowed to lay in and get up when I wanted to. My roommate for most part of the first season was Lawrence Leyton, the magician, his assistant was Julie, she was sharing a cabin with one of the "Champagne dancers". The walls of the cabin were covered in a blue striped carpet, that gave it a very cosy feel.

Lawrence was a great cabin mate, and the best Magician/Hypnotist I ever worked with, he later went on to do several tv shows for Easy jet called fearless flyer, where he would motivate people who were petrified of flying, he helped them to get on an airplane and fly

43

somewhere without the fear. I watched his hypnotic technique and tried it out on a few people on the cruise ship and I managed to Hypnotise all successfully. So never look into my eyes you never know what I'll get you to do!

Rehearsals began, and there were six shows to get right before the passengers would embark in Venice at the end of April. My job was to stage manage these shows to perfection, the sound, light, props, and all the other technical stuff had to be spot on for the show to look good. In fact, the next four seasons I was the only one called back for my growing expertise in these fields. I was good at it. Let me explain why they kept calling me back each season. I knew how to operate the sound mixing desk, that output all the mics, cassettes, and other audio devices into the mix. The Lighting rig, and spotlights. The curtain, all the props on and off stage. I guess I was a Mr continuity man, they could rely on me, I never let them down. I had to move fast, getting mic stands on and off stage, along with magician's props and get back to start the music for the magician, turn the stage lights up, it was very demanding, but I loved it, lots of adrenalin.

This was such an unbelievable part of my life, the food was incredible, on a Friday, evening meal consisted of rainbow trout starter followed by beef wellington and for afters it was baked Alaska, not too shabby, Wednesday night food was Greek food and I love this cuisine Greek salad, Moussaka, Calamari, and all the deserts were so yummy. Food on the La Palma was outstanding and after an evening meal I would get changed and run upstairs for the spectacular show, if you fancied it, the midnight buffet was normally Spaghetti bolognaise or endless pizza, if you had room! I would go down to the nightclub and play pop and dance classics till 2am. My DJ equipment, twin decks and vinyl records were sent by air freight in flight cases to Athens then by lorry to the port of Piraeus. The crew helped me get my stuff onboard and got it all down to the lower decks of the ship. I then unpacked and assembled the sound and light in the nightclub, and we were good to go.

Each week my mum would post me seven-inch vinyl records, the new entries in the chart, so to keep me up to date with the latest charts in England, and I would get them about a week later. The Italian girls loved Level 42, Spandau ballet and Wham, and when I chatted any of them up in the little Italian I had learnt, they would say I was "Sympatico", which basically translates to "nice person". Little did they know, I was a naughty rascal really.

One evening the ship was full of travel agents from Italy and Germany, mainly young women. I stage managed the show upstairs and the cruise director announced the nightclub was now open till the early hours! Well, I ran down to the nightclub and it was absolutely packed solid. I had to run upstairs quickly to change my clothes, I said to one of the waiters please pick a record from my vinyl collection and put it on the turntable and play it, I would be back in five minutes. When I returned, I couldn't believe what was happening. The dancefloor was packed with the most beautiful girls imaginable. They were all gyrating to the beat, and when I looked at the turntable the waiter by mistake, had slipped on the B side of "slightest touch" by five star, the instrumental version, and it was playing at 33rpm, it was supposed to be at 45rpm, so it was a lot slower than it should have been, the ladies on the dancefloor didn't notice a thing, until I changed the song to "Easy lover" by Phil Collins, then the place erupted into an almighty frenzy of body movements that went long into the night.

The weekly cruise on board La Palma began on Saturday in Venice, the passengers embarked at 9am and we set sail at 3pm, with the musicians setting up outside near the Beer Garden and playing for an hour till 4pm.

Sunday was a day at sea, then Monday morning we would squeeze through the Corinth canal and arrive about 1pm in Piraeus, where hopefully I'd pick up my new 7 inch-vinyl records that were posted by my mum the week before and brought onboard upon our arrival via the ship's agent, he would come onboard with all the entertainment staff's mail. It was my job to then distribute it to their cabins below deck. Every Monday I felt like Santa Clause, seeing their smiling faces, getting mail from home meant a lot, I loved being postman.

we would set off at 7pm for Rhodes, out on deck the ships orchestra were playing calypso and merengue tunes, dressed in Hawaiian shirts and white trousers. Overnight the sea would be calm, and we would arrive there 8am Tuesday, we had twelve hours there it was my favourite Greek island, in the old town near the taxi rank there was the Top 3 bar, that still to this day plays my music in the bar and pictures of me adorn the walls. Wednesday morning, we would arrive in Crete leaving at 1pm for Corfu, arriving at 10am Thursday and leaving at 7pm. Friday at 8am we would dock in Dubrovnik leaving at 1pm, then off to Venice arriving 6am Saturday and start all over again.

Every Wednesday was Greek night on board La Palma, the restaurant was decorated in Greek flags, blue and white everywhere, the food was all Greek and I love Greek food, from the moussaka to the feta cheese in the salads, tiny fish deep fried in batter known as whitebait, everything about it I love so much. The show was everything Greek, lifting tables with their teeth to the shouts of "ooopaa" plenty of audience participation and even the captain joined in the dancing. They drew the line when it came to smashing plates, it just wasn't practical on a cruise ship. The Greek night is always a good one, but the night was not finished just yet.

The cruise director announces with a smile "you are all invited down to the nightclub for the Pyjama party but remember entry to the party is by pyjama only, if you don't wear your pyjamas you will not be allowed in!!" I made it quickly down to my cabin and changed into my stockings and suspenders and an all-in-one number that just about hid me meat and two veg, then I stood guard at the bottom of the stairs outside the entrance to the nightclub and encouraged passengers to change into their bedroom gear, and normally when they saw me in the kinky lingerie it would normally do the trick. the sights I have seen on those pyjama nights have been unbelievable but hey, they are the ones on holiday. Hostesses would translate on my microphone the dances that I put on, and the Champagne dancers would get involved too. The Gap band and Oops upside your head was first up with that famous dance being rein acted on the dance floor of the nightclub. We did Nellie the elephant by the Toy dolls, this worked very well, especially when they went backwards. La Bamba was a good one too, it was a good night down in the nightclub.

On Friday afternoon, after we left Dubrovnik there would be a Miss La Palma beauty competition, this would take place outside by the pool bar, music would play and the cruise director would introduce the ladies in there bikinis and onlookers would get a voting slip to cast their vote, the winner would be crowned before Friday night's farewell show, this competition was very competitive and some of the ladies would put a bit of lipstick on or tie back their hair, but it was all done in a good spirit.

Monday nights leaving Piraeus there was no show but in the main lounge, games would be played and this could be very funny indeed, we knew this was coming so Lawrence my cabin mate and the ships fantastic magician was also a professional hypnotist and before the game he met up with a married couple and put them under into a deep trance and instructed them both that they will be determined to win the game that involved a human version of musical chairs, so rather than using chairs they used men.

This was so funny, the focus and determination of them both. They elbowed and pulled and pushed others out of their path to get to their goal, and yes, they both won a bottle of champagne each, just shows you how powerful Hypnosis is.

Tuesday on the cruise itinerary was my favourite day, 2pm till 7pm we were in Rhodes and as soon as La Palma docked the entertainment staff was off to Elli beach, always packed with sun worshippers, from the dock it was a walk of around 20 minutes, passing the historic old town and the harbour full of yachts, boats, fishing vessels, and excursion specials, these fun boats would take you on day trips to Turkey or up the coast to Lindos.

Lindos is one of the most beautiful places I have ever visited, stunning small white houses on the side of a mountain that leads down to an inviting beach with clear sea water and golden sands.

Elli beach is just outside Rhodes new town and has a far busier beach, thousands of sun beds and looky looky men selling watermelon and drinks, topless sunbathing everywhere, and that was just the blokes! And along the beach road, bars catering for the Irish, Scandinavian, Bavarian, and English drinkers.

Depending how hot the temperature was, would depend on when I would make my way to the Top 3 Bar, I couldn't stand it too hot, so when it was scorchio, you would find me there.

Spiro is the owner of the bar, and he is a great man, his wife Maria was special too, the loveliest of ladies. In 1986 I provided the bar with all the latest songs from the English chart, Rock classics and party mixes. Good music makes a bar and Spiro was very grateful for my tapes. If you fancy a beer in there one day and you are in Rhodes town, it is next to the taxi rank, check it out, its nice in there, with lovely people. And the music isn't bad either.

All the entertainment staff would eventually end up in the top 3 bar on route to La Palma, we all had to be back on board by 6,30pm, or we were in big shit, so from four, musicians, singers and dancers from the ship would gather and get slightly inebriated, then at six it would be a drunken walk back to the ship in the evening heat. God, I loved Tuesday and the Greek island of Rhodes.

At the beginning of the cruise season 87 we joined the La Palma in Plymouth in March 1987, it coincided with the Herald of free enterprise ferry disaster, which killed almost 200. We sailed the next day. The newly embarked passengers must have been a little nervous. We had started show rehearsals for the coming season at Butlins in Torquay a week earlier and were ready for the coming season. We will be heading for Lisbon, Gibraltar, Tunis, Madeira, and the Canary Islands, then In April start our regular Greek island itinerary. At the end of September, we would have a few charters visiting Turkey, Cyprus, Egypt, Malta, and Israel.

Gibraltar was a great place to visit, very English, The pubs the food. Even red telephone boxes and British bobbies. Everyone spoke English and I remember visiting the Barbary apes via the cable car. They nicked my bloody camera the little bleeders. Good job it was an old one, and no pictures had been taken yet. Once those apes snatch it, you are not getting it back, they tried to eat it, must have thought it was a cake until they bite into it. When they realise its inedible, they throw it down the cliff. Charming.

Madeira is beautiful, we had many overnight stops at the port there. Its famous for Cake, wine and on New Year's Eve they have a world-famous firework display. In the harbour is the Beatles yacht and lots of turtles can be seen swimming round it. This is the birthplace of Cristiano Ronaldo, the greatest of all time.

The Canary Islands are Spanish owned and very much all the same, Tenerife is my favourite one and Lanzarote has two sides with different climates. One of the volcanos there is always bubbling, and if you go to the top, the tourist guide will show you how hot it is underfoot by frying an egg on the rocks there.

Egypt was an eye opener, poverty, disease, affluent apartments, and shit holes side by side. The marketplace stinking of fish, flies all over the place. The Cairo Museum was fantastic, full of actual artefacts of Tutankhamun, or maybe it was the air conditioning and lack of flies that made me enjoy the museum so much. The Pyramids are awesome, and the sphynx is slowly crumbling. I did attempt to crouch down and shuffle into the centre of the Pyramid, but just after a few feet, I had to back out. It was very claustrophobic, so I settled for a camel ride.

Israel, and the port of Ashdod, talk about chalk and cheese, the streets are clean and have a Mediterranean feel about them. The first thing I noticed was the ladies, wow so beautiful, I would go as far to say the most beautiful I have seen, and because they are obliged to do national service, they are in uniform and armed with a machine gun. I rest my case. Security is high understandably, it felt like you were being watched all the time, but considering the country's history, it is a way of life there.

Sixteen of the entertainment team hired 4 Mercedes taxis for a day long tour, four of us in each taxi and around 40 miles into Jerusalem, It was a comfortable air conditioned car and we set off for Bethlehem and it took about an hour to pull up outside the military police station that protected the church in the town of Bethlehem, inside it contained the tiny church where it is believed is the exact place where Jesus was born, we all queued up, and when it was my turn I bent down and kissed the golden coloured star on the floor, wow I felt very emotional, I felt privileged, and it wasn't the last time I kissed the star, I visited that place another couple of occasions. Each time it felt very spiritual, a warm sort of glow came over me. Israel is a very holy place and well worth visiting, one of my favourite places.

Close by was a "Superstore" for everything nativity or Holy, I bought a nativity scene of Mary and Joseph and baby Jesus in the manger, carved from wood, still got it on my mantlepiece today. There were rosary beads, holy water, framed pictures of the nativity, it was a store totally dedicated to Christianity.

Next stop was Mount Olive, the taxis stopped here for the great view of Jerusalem, when you next watch BBC news, and they are reporting from Jerusalem they always use this image for the backdrop, it features the Blue Mosque and Wailing wall in the distance, it was a great potential picture. We all got out of the taxis and took a few shots, including a group shot of the entertainment staff, taken by one of the taxi drivers. There was such a great atmosphere among the group.

The taxis set off again and headed down a hill towards the occupied territories, suddenly school children started throwing rocks and boulders onto the road, big boulders the size of football's, three taxis got through this bombardment, but our car was stuck, the road was blocked at the front and the back of the Mercedes and the atmosphere in the taxi changed, it was very quiet, the Jewish driver got on his radio and informed the authorities of our situation. We looked round at each other trying to laugh it off nervously,

Within minutes the Israeli army were on the scene and several jumped from there jeeps and with batons in hand started to hit the children demanding they clear the road. We watched from the taxi as the kids did as they were told, and very soon our road was clear. With a jeep escort we carried on down the hill to be met by a large group of Palestinians gesticulating angrily at our taxi as we passed, a few expletives were directed at our Israeli escorts too.

Once down at the bottom of the hill the driver dropped us off at the main gates of Jerusalem and said he would pick us up at 4pm to take us back to La Palma. That would give us plenty of time to explore the sights and get a bit of lunch. The wailing wall was impressive, very well guarded and at the wall itself Rabi's and other Jewish people writing notes and posting in the cracks of the wall and praying that their wishes would come true. The blue mosque was a short walk away and worth a look, but I didn't go inside, which I do regret now, as these two places are especially important for the respective religions. The church of the holy sepulchre was far more interesting to me, being a catholic, this is the rock where Jesus was crucified, and the tomb where Jesus rose from the dead, I noticed that it was guarded by Greek orthodox priests and had a strong spiritual feeling about it. It is a very impressive and holy City; I loved my visits there; Israel is one of my favourite places beyond a shadow of a doubt.

Thursday night was the "Around the world" show, during the rehearsals I suggested as part of the finale we should sing "We are the world" which was greeted with a lot of positivity, although they decided each member of the entertainment team would sing a line, including me! Then they asked "Noel, can you sing?" I looked at them in disbelief. "Is the Pope a catholic?" I retorted. They all laughed and selected my line in the song, it would be "And so we all must lend a helping hand" I smashed it! And my line and the song kept in all season long.

I was lucky, I didn't get sea-sick but some of the dancers would turn green at the first indication of rough seas. The Bay of Biscay was always rough and, on this occasion, very rough, the ships stewards would line the corridors with paper sick containers, and if you did venture out of your cabin, those containers were what you aimed for.

I was up on the Casino and boutique deck, not many passengers about but the ship was going forward like a corkscrew, try not to visualise this movement I don't want my readers to hurl. The front of the ship was being lifted high on the waves and then smashing down hard, shuddering and creaking as it progressed through the water, my senses were heightened, so I could feel everything that was going on, the ship was listing from one side to the other, very slowly, but this was causing chairs to roll form one side of the room to the other, this wasn't helping the situation. Behind me a muffled scream rang out and when I turned an elderly lady was pinned between the rows of slot machines, one side had broken away from the iron girders they were attached to, very quickly staff came to her rescue and helped her free, she was bruised and shaken, and the captain offered her a free cruise in the summer.

One of my friends on board was a fantastic impressionist and singer, Frank Ford was his name and he told me of a story of when he was going through the Bay of Biscay on a ship called The Black watch. It had hit very bad weather and the waves were ginormous, all the staff and crew were shitting themselves. A freak wave hit the bridge and smashed the windows, setting off the ships automatic alarms to abandon ship. The auto announcement said, "Please go to your muster stations and lower the lifeboats abandon ship" This message was automatic, but the waves were so big there was no way a lifeboat could be lowered. Can you imagine the panic throughout the ship. But here is the punchline. One of the singers in the entertainment's team went down six decks to get his music from his cabin. Is that crazy or what? He was more worried about his music, than his own life. Just to explain, "music" is the parts that you hand to a musician in the ship's orchestra. The Piano part, Drums, Bass, Lead guitar, they all have a part. All singers have music, and it is there little baby, so was he right?

Most of the time the ship sails through to the next port without a stir, the sea is flat like a ginormous bath and during the day the sky is blue, in the evening you look up to see the night sky emblazoned with stars. Occasionally the seas get angry, and it is very scary, I wouldn't be going down six decks to retrieve my precious stuff. Save your life first.

American passengers are the best, first they tip, and I mean they tip large, it's just the way they do things in the states. I would take groups of them round the islands on scooters, and they loved it. At the end of the cruise, they would all chip in and tip, very generous people. Some of them are very strange, one lady from the states asked me where I was from? When I said London, she said "Do you know the Queen?" another one looked at me straight in the eye and asked me "What time is the midnight buffet?" I told her it was at 12 O'clock and she shuffled away quite happy.

One year I arranged for my sister Lorraine, her husband George and daughter Irene, (who was two years old) and my Mum to spend a week onboard La Palma, My Mum hadn't been out of the British Isles before, so this was a big deal for her, I am so proud I paid for her time on-board La Palma she had a great holiday. I wouldn't be here if it wasn't for her. Working hard as a dinner lady to afford my first lot of DJ equipment. My mum had sacrificed everything for me, and now, in a small way I was helping her have the best holiday ever, it is what a son should do.

The family flew into Venice, stayed overnight, and came onboard Saturday morning, they were allocated their rooms, my mum shared with young Irene while Lorraine and George had the cabin next door. My mum's face was a picture she looked so happy, the next seven nights they were all spoilt rotten, by the Greek crew, and entertainment staff. The head dancer Allison Jay paid special attention to young Irene, playing with her at every opportunity.

It cannot be stressed highly enough how my sister Lorraine and her husband George have helped me throughout my life, with work, and helping me buy new DJ equipment to stay up to date. I thank them both for their love and generosity and I am forever grateful.

We all went sightseeing on Monday, visiting the acropolis in Athens, and on Tuesday after a bit of shopping and a meal we ended up in the Top 3 bar, Spiro bought my mum a bunch of flowers and he wouldn't let us buy a drink all afternoon, this is the kindness of Greek people, they have great respect and humility.

Saturday soon came round, the family had a fantastic week on board, it was an emotional send off, Lorraine, George, and young Irene had a great time, my mum watched all the shows I stage managed I could tell she was proud of her son, entertaining all the passengers. This is what I will do for the rest of my life. Entertain. I am glad she got to see this; it was the best thing I have ever done for my mum.

I was 25 years of age and the fun and games I had on the La Palma was unbelievable, I was no Peter Andre by any stretch of the imagination, but what I did have was the gift of the gab, The Captain used to call me the "Chief Kamaki" which in Greek translates as "spear" in other words, I was fishing with my spear and having lots of luck with the ladies. My true intention when boarding the ship at the beginning of each season was to find a girlfriend among the entertainment staff, and stick with her throughout the summer, but this never happened for a multitude of reasons, in fact it did happen once, with a dancer from Birmingham her name was Louisa and she was so bubbly and fun to be around, unfortunately it lasted only six weeks, she was a bit of a flirt and I caught her snogging one of the officers! but it was a great six weeks as far as I was concerned, you see Louisa apart from being very fit and beautiful, she was a very bendy woman, a contortionist in fact, and she could get in more positions than Georgie Best. Yes, it was a very good six weeks. While it lasted.

There was another Dancer that seduced me one night after I had finished my set in the nightclub, her name was Louise, with very curly mousey coloured hair, she had a stunning smile and a great kiss. She waited for me outside the nightclub and wallop she literally jumped on me. I had no clue this was going to happen. And it didn't happen again, maybe she needed a cuddle, but I was more than happy to accommodate. We both ended up outside at the front of the ship, a bit like the famous scene from Titanic, even though that film wasn't even being filmed yet. It was dark around 3am and we were having a bit of a canoodle, it was just a bit of fun, and I think alcohol had something to do with it. Next morning, I was summoned to the staff captain's office, who was watching mine and Louise antics from the bridge in the early hours, he smiled as he gave me a three thousand drachma fine. To be honest it was well worth the fine. Alas, I never canoodled with Louise again.

On Friday night's I would help the photographer, for a small fee, I would dress in a gorilla costume and pose for pictures with passengers as they left the restaurant after their farewell dinner, The Gorilla outfit was very realistic and caused women to scream uncontrollably once they had seen me in full view. When they got to the top of the stairs, I would grab them and lift them in the air to even more screams, with the photographer getting some very uncompromising shots, in the darkroom later he shared with me a picture of a young Italian lady he developed but was not going to be displayed in the ship's gallery! The lady was wearing a very short mini-skirt and once I had picked her up and pointed her towards the lens of the camera, it was very clear in the developed picture she had no panties on! And her "secret garden" was there for all the world to see!

I continued being chief Kamaki and had naughty adventures all over the ship including the Ironing room, the nudist deck, the hairdresser's salon, and the ships theatre dressing room.

The nudist deck was the last resort for nookie, if I couldn't find a place to go with my lady friend. It was situated directly under the ships thunnel, high on the top deck of the ship. In the early hours of the morning, it was a bit windy and small pieces of ash would land in that area 24/7. It was visited by the ships fire wardens, who walked around the ship to check for any potential fire risks all through the night, like the ash coming out the thunnel. The main attraction of the nudist deck for me was looking up and seeing billions of stars in the night sky, it is something spectacular on a clear night. But the hazard of messing around up there was the unwelcomed visit of the fire warden, so timing was very important. If I got caught with my trousers down by the fire warden he would report me to the staff captain, and another wad of drachma notes would end up in the staff captain's hand.

The nudist deck was used by the ships officers when it was docked, and no passengers were on board. Not for naturism but cooking a whole lamb on a spit with hot charcoal underneath, and a very long process would begin. This mainly would happen at easter time. This is the most holy part of the year for Greeks and all these traditions take place on this weekend. The entertainment staff were invited to this special gathering and a few free beers were handed around. It was all very nice and watching the lamb getting cooked was very mouth-watering indeed. The ships chefs were turning the lamb occasionally and sprinkling herbs and seasoning as it rotated, when it eventually was ready the ship's captain took the brains of the lamb and eat it, as is tradition. It is meant to be an aphrodisiac, so our dancers better watch out tonight. When I tasted this lamb, that had been cooking since early morning, it is the best food I have ever eaten. It melted in my mouth; it was succulent and along with the added ingredients during the cooking process it was out of this world. I will never forget it as long as I live.

The best night that season was on a pyjama night and I was dressed in my usual stockings and suspenders, as the passengers came down into the nightclub, two young ladies from Belgium came down the stairs and burst into laughter when they saw my kinky costume, I suggested they return to their cabin and change into something they might wear in bed, fair play to them, they went back to their cabin and when they returned they were both wearing very sexy lingerie, mainly black in colour, but a splash of red lace. They were wearing very large smiles on their faces. Later that evening when the nightclub closed. My cabin was all mine, the photographer was sleeping in his girlfriend's cabin. So, not for the last time, we had a *manage a trois* situation going on and we gladly swapped lingerie, eventually.

Back in the day, every time I heard the name Damian, I immediately thought of the horror movie "The Omen" and the murderous child from hell, and that would automatically link me to the new-born son of Del boy and Raquel in the sit-com "only fools and horses" oh no, not anymore, now when I hear the name Damian I think of my young and very good-looking cabin mate on La Palma, what a formidable pair we were with the Ladies. The thing was, Damian was the drummer in the ship's orchestra, and he could pull a bird. He didn't have to say a word, ladies would literally throw themselves at him, he was a cross between James Dean and George Clooney and I am not joking, he was only 21 and he was going to have one hell of a time. We got on like a house on fire, and silly me decided to set him a challenge on who could get the most "girl friends" over the course of the season so we kept a league table, and it was all done just for a bit of fun really.

It was a normal day in Corfu until Damian informed me his sister and her mate were going to meet up with him this very day and he invited me along for the company. We arrived around midday at the port and went down onto the quayside and there was Damian's sister and her mate, WOW they were like super-models absolutely stunning, both six feet tall with long legs up to their armpits, we greeted them warmly and we decided to get mopeds and set off to a fantastic beach I had been to many times before, it was about 45 minutes away and the girls wanted to relax and get some rays so this was a perfect place for that. What happened next was quite unbelievable and very weird.

This beautiful, secluded bay with white sand, clear water with tiny fish swimming around our feet, the sky was blue with the sweltering sun shining its heat down on us as we decided to climb the rocks at the far end of the bay, this led us to a secret tiny lagoon area out of site from the others on the beach. Sally (Damian's sister) and Sam (short for Samantha) had brought Damian a gift from home, a small supply of black Marijuana, He was delighted, Damian loved a joint. It was quickly made into a long thin joint and was passed around, my first go and I was out of my nut, the two beauties stood up and unfastened their bikini tops revealing the most beautiful breasts I have ever seen in my life, someone pinch me, is this a dream? Am I hallucinating? I looked at Damian who was giggling like a small boy, I turned around and the girls were completely naked! bloody hell! I was acting so cool, as though this sort of thing happens to me all the time, "are you coming in Noel?" Sally said as they both lowered themselves into the water, she didn't have to ask me twice and I thought what the heck, let's go commando! My little willy was revealed briefly as I sauntered into the pool, very soon Damian jumped in giggling even more hysterically and was soon canoodling with his sister's mate Sam. I told you this was weird, while treading water Sally swam over to me, although the water was cold, she was steaming hot, and she planted a kiss on my lips, I can't tell you what was happening under the water, but to this day, it was the closest I got to heaven.

On another day I got off the ship at my favourite place Rhodes and as usual headed for Eli beach, it was another boiling hot day and when I arrived, I saw the elderly Greek lady who hired me one of her sun loungers and sun umbrella, I placed my towel down and started to apply factor thirty onto my already Sunkissed body (lobster red).

Next to me, just a metre away was a Scandinavian lady prostrate on her bed, blonde hair, with a deep brown tan that was glistening in the sunshine, she was topless with just a G-string covering her modesty. Next to her was a window cleaner spray container, full of cold water, she was using it to spray herself to cool down in the extreme heat. She looked up and saw me looking in her direction, "Hello how are you?" I said, and she replied in very good English "Very well, are you enjoying your holiday?" I explained I was working on a cruise ship and would be leaving that evening for Crete; she sat up and we began chatting like we were old friends. "Can I get you a beer?" "Yes please, a cold one would be really nice of you" she said politely. I found out she was from Stockholm in Sweden and on holiday on her own, she had the most beautiful blue eyes and after a few more beers she lay back on the lounger and asked, "would you spray me with this to cool me down?" as she passed me the half-emptied spray gun. My aim was accurate, and I conservatively started with her flat tummy, her eyes were closed but I could see she was loving this cool spray on her skin, I couldn't resist it the boobs were next, her tongue was now gently licking her lips, I think I've pulled! We staggered back to her hotel room and got up to all sorts of mischief, in the shower, on the balcony, I was such a stud back then.

we had a few drinks at the Top 3 bar, and I took her on board for some more fun, with just enough time to say goodbye and escort her off, before La Palma sailed. The following day………..

I was having a drink at the beer garden, which I loved to do, it was quality beer imported from Munich and traditionally it went along with sausage, bread roll and mustard. On the other side of the bar, I was joined by an Austrian lady, very slim and tall with natural blonde hair, and a nice smile, "good morning" I said raising my glass of spaten beer "Prost" I heard her reply, which is German for cheers. I asked if I could join her, and she nodded. Boom! I've pulled. I spent that afternoon having fun with Paula, chatting away. I said that I was working that night in the nightclub would she like to come down and meet me there after the show. She said "Yes I look forward to it" in her German accent. I said my auf wiedershen and looked forward to the evening ahead.

I performed by duties that evening as stage manager for the evening show, went to my cabin and changed and went down to the nightclub. Paula was there waiting for me. She looked gorgeous, short white mini skirt, with an ultraviolet blue top. I got us drinks and was counting down the clock to finish the night. When it eventually came to an end we went to my cabin and what followed was a great night of love making. She was a very loving young woman. I left her alone in the cabin for two minutes while I went to the ships kitchens to see what I could get. I opened the freezer door and found a large bunch of white seedless grapes, I tasted one, they were ice cold, very sweet and juicy. When I returned with the grapes to my cabin, she was naked in my bed, the bedclothes were to one side revealing her beautiful body, long legs, tiny boobs, she was a stunner. The grapes were freezing cold, and I began to burst them all over her body, the juice from the grapes were licked off with care. She reacted very responsively, and it was a wonderful night. I wish I kept in touch with Paula she was the best.

The league table at the end of the ten-month season was 14 each.

I would like to thank Arthur Belmont, Roger Kendrick, but most of all Frank and Allison Connor for helping me in fulfilling my dreams on board La Palma, they taught me about lighting, sound, props, and the continuity of a show. They did it very professionally and made it so much fun, thank you from the bottom of my heart.

FOR YOUR INFORMATION It might be a shock to you all, but I have a mental illness, it's called **depression**, sometimes I am fine, but when I suffer it is difficult to control. I want to put this out there because sometimes I might seem a bit quiet or shy, other times I am very anxious, and my mind works overtime. Please try and understand I am not the only one, many people suffer in silence, I get very tired and lethargic, my flat is an absolute mess, but I am here writing a book, and have my own radio station, so I do not want sympathy, I want you to understand that I have an illness and some of you reading this will also suffer, so thanks for understanding.

I also suffer from **psoriasis;** I can't believe I spelt it correctly! This effects my skin making it itchy and very dry, I use creams to moisten the skin otherwise it goes flaky, it stops me from wearing shorts and short sleeve shirts because it can become unsightly. It dents my confidence and effects my pulling power, once again do not feel sorry for me just realise why I am wearing trousers and long sleeve shirt on a boiling hot day.

I am glad I got that off my chest now we can get back to the book.

I started a sound cloud account so you could catch up with radio shows that I have recorded and uploaded, the way to tune in is go to Sound cloud and search for bermondseysnumberone

If you would like to tune in and listen to Bermondsey radio LIVE 10.30am Sunday morning, google Bermondsey Radio and click on the link

Or you can download the free android app on the play store, just search for Bermondsey radio, you might like to join our Facebook page just search Bermondsey radio.

The Lilliput Hall otherwise known as "The Lill" the best pub I ever worked

Chapter five

1990... back to blighty

September 1990, they threw me off the ship in the port of Piraeus, it's a shocker, isn't it? I demanded my own cabin, as it was written in my contract, they didn't like my demand, so I was history, despite the fact I worked there for 5 years, giving everything for the success of the shows. My heart was broken and devastated and while I packed away my DJ equipment I was in a state of shock. The La Palma sailed away without me for the first time in five years, I stood on the quay side and pulled out a union flag from my bag and waved it defiantly with tears rolling down my cheeks. The best part of my life was floating away. Meanwhile on board all my friends on board cheered and waved me off from the back of the ship. I loved every moment on board, it was time to move on and fly home to Blighty.

Well, what am I going to do now? I just had to pick myself up, dust myself down and prove them all wrong again. Day jobs included knocking on doors and selling sky dishes, working as a salesman for a British rail nationwide parcel delivery service called Track 29, my brother-in-law Georgie Archer owned the franchise.

I was deejaying for the Fisher club at the original clubhouse in Salter Road, Joey Herd and his wife Carole run the bar and they were fantastic to me, and fisher had a great football team then. Their captain Dennis Sharpe led great players like Bobby Shiners, Peter Hawkes, Billy Bowles to name but a few. Dogan Arif was the manager and owned Le connoisseur restaurant on the Old Kent Road, a great place to go on a

Sunday night after the pubs had closed. We used to fall out of there in the wee small hours, there was no way I would make it into work Monday morning, yet again.

I occasionally helped with the stadium announcing at Fisher from the main stand, welcoming the fans to the match, reading out the line ups before 3pm, and at half time the scores from the other matches being played on the day including how Millwall were getting on. I played DJ sets many times in the clubhouse, it had a modern dance floor with a up to date lighting rigg in the ceiling, I would provide the tunes after the match on cd, vinyl records were now on the way out so I was changing my music library to cd's, this would take a while but because the audio was much better, all deejays were doing the same as me. Sunday afternoon's I was resident DJ in the Stanley arms in Southwark Park Road, my mates would be out most Sunday's, Albert, Gary, Scooter and Harry Ball, his mum and dad, and Terry and Sheila Webb. Always a great drinking session on a Sunday and later in the afternoon lots of dancing, when all the ladies would come in.
I used to love playing in the Alscot pub for the late Tommy Ball, God rest his soul, and the lovely Glenda, that was a special boozer lots of dancing with classic seventies tunes and they were so nice to work for.

In the nineties I worked New year's eve mostly in an Italian restaurant in Locksbottom called Mama Mia's, it was a long slim room, I would set up just inside the door what would normally be there cloakroom, it was now a DJ booth, at the time I also presented Karaoke and it proved popular with the dinners, at around 10pm I would go into party mode with all the classics till I did the countdown followed by the chimes from Big Ben, I worked there consecutively till 98, we always had a great party there till 2am including a special twelve inch version of La Bamba and the guests would form a long line and naughtily gate crash the restaurant 3 doors down the high street, dancing around the tables and retuning to our place laughing their heads off.

When I started playing music in 1979 It was Vinyl 7 and 12-inch records, singles and extended mixes and albums, in the late seventies they started to issue coloured vinyl records, Squeeze had many of their singles released in various colours, pink for Up the junction and red clear for Slap and tickle, The Police issued message in a bottle on green. Five years later the CD was born.

My CD collection begun with Michael McDonald's greatest hits, followed by Daryl Hall and John Oats greatest hits, Dire straits, Jon, and Vangelis, soon I had hundreds of them and invested in a twin CD player, before long, my twin decks (turntables) was not getting on the van, vinyl was dead. CD was the new king.

But before we had time to say Come on Eileen, the Mp3 player was born, with thousands of tracks stored on a device the size of a packet of cigarettes. But hold on, everything has changed again, now in 2022 it's all about downloads of Mp3's, I preferred Flac files, they were larger files with more digital information on them. Flac files had superior audio and when using a midi controller through RCF powered speakers it produced the most superb sound. My priceless record collection, 10,000 strong, are now all on my laptop, with the best sound possible. This means I have had to change my collection three times since 1979, Cd's, MP3's and FLAC's, what is the next technology that will replace this one? Only time will reveal the next big thing. I am ready for the next technology; I am not hanging my headphones up just yet. I am taking bookings for 2023, it will be my forty fourth year of playing music.

In no particular order, I am going to name some of the venues that I have played this past forty-odd years, apologies if I miss you out, but you mustn't have been very good. The number one pub, The Lilliput Hall and always will be. The Swan & Sugarloaf was great fun with

Albert Lawson and Bobby Crawford. The Alscot, great times, The George Camilla Road some great parties, The Ship St Marys' with Del boy and Ann on a Sunday fantastic, The Stanley arms classic times, The Blue Anchor, The Gregorian Arms, The Clarence, The Kings Arms, The Fisher Club, Harry's bar & the executive suites Millwall F.C, Bromley FC, Wade hall, The Felton club, The old Justice, The Crown, The Boatman, Cock and Monkey, Claridge's hotel, The Dorchester, Jumeirah Carlton Tower, The St James tavern when Colin had it, The Foresters, The Raymouth tavern, The Neptune, Ship Aground, The Fleece, The Raven, MV La Palma, The Pride of London riverboat, The Downtown restaurant, The ship of York, The Windsor, The Beehive Walworth Road, The Beehive Eltham, The Charcoal Burner Sidcup, The Bulls head, Mama Mia's Locksbottom, The House of commons, The Bermondsey Carnival, The Yorkshire grey Eltham, The Henry Cooper, The Kings on the Rye. Sidcup golf club, Chislehurst golf club, The Wellington druid street, The Danish club Knightsbridge, Lake Como Italy (2 weddings) Spa Road library hall, The Beormand centre, Fisher Downside club, Guys Tower, Phoenix club, The Ramblers rest, The Beaverwood club, The Glebe sports ground, Dartford FC, Bromley cricket club, St Joseph's RC school gomm road. The Moat Wrotham, Bromley court hotel, Hilton downtown, Spa Hotel Tunbridge Wells, Thomas A Beckett, The Park lane Hilton, Asylum tavern, Queen Victoria, Queen Vic pages walk, The Surdock club, Southwark Park tavern, Southwark Park club, The Old Bank there have been thousands of other venues, but I think you get the idea, from the poshest doo's to the tenants halls of South east London, no airs and graces, just a bloody good knees up, that's for sure.

I have been very lucky to have played warm up act for several musical stars including Chas & Dave (five times) The Real Thing (twice) Alexander O'Neal (twice) Rose Royce, Heatwave, Stacey Solomon, The Proclaimers, Brian May (Queen), Bill Wyman's Rhythm kings, Dave Edmunds, Darts, The Blockheads, Glen Tilbrook, Chris Difford, Joe Brown, Lee Thomson (Madness) Paul Carrack, Nine below zero and many more. But although it was a great privilege to share the stage with these fine performers and play at the finest hotels, my finest work and bread and butter is playing for local people, it always will be.

On February 19th, 1994, my mum passed away after a short illness, it was cancer, and the McMillan nurses did their best to help her right to the end. I miss my mum so much, she brought me up with terrific values and respect for others, she gave me everything, when really, she had nothing at all, It was my mum who helped me by buying my first lot of DJ equipment, without this generous act none of the above would have happened, no weddings, no birthdays, no Bermondsey radio, and no book. So, thank you mum, from the bottom of my heart, until we meet again, love you always Noel.

My mum came from Mulhuddart, Blanchardstown about 12 miles outside Dublin, she moved to England in 1958 with my dad and sisters Breda and Lill, my sister Lill passed away a few years ago and was always lovely to me, and I miss her very much. My mum worked at Television centre at the BBC wood lane for several years and at my two schools as a dinner lady. She was the best.

In the 90's I worked for Dockhead cars, mini cabbing in a white Vauxhall cavalier, I would get up early in the morning and work through till mid-afternoon. In the fog and the snow, traffic, and the mechanical breakdowns. Patrick Spring was the owner, we all called him Patsy and to me he was a very nice man, a funny man with a big heart, especially when he would give me jobs to Heathrow for £30 a pop. There was so many characters and dodgy cars all in one place.

The drivers were all well known in the area for their eccentricities, we had "Charlie overcoat", who wore the same overcoat for years on end, he smoked roll ups in his car while passengers were alongside him, if you were lucky, he would let you lower the window, to allow the smoke to escape. "Billy Kiptanooie" had no teeth, a lovely gummy smile and drove an antique Ford Sierra, he also chain smoked. And there was "Dick" who would occasionally work as the controller, but drove a clapt-out old Ford Granada, another smoker and he needed a good wash! Bernie Shorter was a proper bread and butter; he was very sophisticated and classy; he had a fountain of sports knowledge which always made me laugh. The legendary Palmer brothers including Jimmy, God rest his soul. They were always fun to be around. I organised social events for Dockhead cars, we went ten pin bowling up at Surrey Quays, I was useless, but it was a good night out with a few beers and laughs. I arranged for us to all go for a Christmas drink at the Downtown restaurant in Odessa Street. It was brilliant, we had a Marti Pellow soundalike, I think I helped him out with his performance they tell me, I can't remember a thing about the night I was rotten as a pear.

Dockhead cars had some cool celebrity customers because it was positioned next to some very expensive apartments on the river around Shad Thames, belonging to Matt and Luke Goss, Clive James, Marc Almond, Mike Stevenson (rugby league), it was quite fun having a chat with them as they sat in the back of my Vauxhall Cavalier, dropping them off all over London.

I got the runs for "The Knowledge" and decided to give it a go. I went to the carriage office and was told by the officer to go out and learn the streets of London and come back when you think you know them. I had a basic knowledge, but there was so much to learn, this was going to be tricky. I met up with my friend Ginger Crawley in Blackheath who sold me his moped for £200, it was an old machine, but he assured me it was a great little runner. I drove it back to Rudge house confidently and parked it up in the flats and hoped it would still be there the next day.

I went out on my first run Manor house station to Gibson square in the pouring rain, in a wetproof mac and leggings and was soaked to the skin before I got to London bridge station. I hadn't gone two miles and I was disheartened. I had a crash helmet on, the visa was steaming up. I finally arrived at Manor house after driving very carefully. Right, here goes, I set off and within a hundred yards the moped breaks down, I am thinking to myself, why me? So, I start to free wheel down green lanes, but soon I was pushing the bike all down through the city, down Moorgate, over London bridge and left into Duke Street hill as I get just outside the London Dungeon another motorbike rider pulls in front of me, gets off his bike "can I help?" he asked. To be honest I was exhausted and wet to the bone and any help at this point was gratefully accepted. It seemed like I had been pushing the moped for twenty miles. I had set off at 4pm and it was now 11.30pm. He looked over my moped very quickly and turned a switch and then turned the key. It started immediately, He explained he turned the spare petrol tank on, and I was good to go. I almost cried, but instead I laughed, and so did he. I had just pushed that thing for hours thinking it was broken, and all I needed was to top it up, or realise to switch on the spare tank. The Moped was sold the next day and that was my one and only run I attempted. I don't think I was cut out to be a black cab driver.

I worked in the Stanley Pub in the nineties, it was a lovely pub and Sunday afternoons would be packed, we would have some great parties from 2pm till 8pm, lots of golden oldies were played "American pie" "Where do you go to my lovely?" "Aint no pleasing you" you would always find the same people in the same corner of the pub, Tommy Sollis, Harry Ball, Albert Lawson, Gary Lambert, David Ford, Terry Webb (God rest his soul) and his wife Sheila, and they were joined by Donna Lawson (Alberts wife) and all the other wives as the afternoon wore on. Sometimes I look back and think wow those were great times, I don't think we really realised how good they were, till there no longer there.

The St George's tavern in Camilla Road (The George) was a complete nuthouse, owned by the magnificent Jeff & June, who both have passed away. I played music there every second Friday and the odd Saturday night when I didn't have a gig of my own, this was a very patriotic pub and always busy at the weekend, If England were playing football, it would be packed solid. The girls loved to dance in there, specially the Hvid sisters Cindy, Alex and Vikki, all beautiful young ladies, they would always jump up on the stage and request a song for their mum and dad, and of course I would always oblige. Lovely people. SOS band, Rod Stewart, or Lionel Richie would be their favourites.

One night a fella walked in the pub while I was playing the tunes and started firing a handgun randomly, all the girls, and some of the blokes ran for cover, into the toilets, under tables. He was chased outside by the Millwall boys and given a jolly good hiding, he ended up in Guys hospital in intensive care, the moral of this story, never mess with Millwall! Or Bermondsey's number one DJ when he's playing the outer bounds. (sounds)

The Ship St Mary's church street, next to Rotherhithe tunnel, along salter road, and chuck a left, was a fantastic pub Del Boy and Anne run this pub very well indeed, I worked there Sunday afternoons, and it was absolutely packed every Sunday, the beautiful barmaids were Jan Perkins, Elaine Turner, Eileen Sullivan, Carole Bryan Tucker, and the one with the sexy lips Angie Stewart. These barmaids had great personalities and you would never be bored in their company.

The food they would put on the bar on a Sunday lunch was the best I have ever seen, 12 noon and there would be plates of prawns, cockles, mussels, and whelks, alongside cheddar cheese and biscuits. Then at 2pm plates of roast potatoes covered in salt would be spread all round the horseshoe shape bar, and finally at 4pm Chinese spareribs, prawn balls and miniature pancake rolls with sweet and sour sauce, fantastic. There was no need to go home for Sunday roast, so many regulars would be in there all day drinking and nibbling at the bar food, and along with myself, playing the tunes it was a winning formula, the pub was packed every weekend. Take note, Bermondsey publicans.

One afternoon there was the most incredible punch up in the pub, they tried to calm down one of the men who lost his temper, but it made it worse, they ushered him out one door and thought they had calmed the situation, within seconds he came back hurtling through the side door, his face red with rage, well he hit this guy so hard with one punch he knocked the fella spark out!, his mates carried him out of the pub and got him a mini cab home, meanwhile back in the pub everything was back to normal, all laughing and joking again as if nothing had happened, only in Bermondsey. On great nights the late great Joycie Bryan would take the mic from me and would sing so wonderfully and with such vigour, she always warmed the cockles of my heart, and we all miss her very much.

It is amazing these days how people ask for requests, some come up to me in 2022 and point their smart phone at me and ask if I can play it for them, so they want me to see they have a smart phone, lucky them, and they then expect me to read what is on the screen, er excuse me but why can't they just say "can you play Candy by Cameo please?" Then the ones that assume you have access to the internet and can stream any song ever released, well, nope I haven't got internet connection and I only buy my tracks, and never stream, that soon stops them in their tracks. Others will ask for a song, then come back after five minutes and say, "Where's my song mate?" they have no chance of me playing that song now. You have to be a certain type of person to be a good deejay, firstly you have to be determined to prove them all wrong, generous with the music that you play, never play your own songs, always play what they want to hear, always play from the heart and not to the beat, always play to the girls, they always start the dancing and will be joined by the men last knockings. Play the music loud and with confidence, always use the best audio equipment, the sound is vital. Go for the jugular, don't let them rest, and use the microphone to show the audience that you are more excited than they are, cajole and persuade and never sit down, now let's get this party started.

As Party's go, they don't come much bigger than the millennium party, and in 1999 they were all after me to play at their shindig, finally a local businessman (J.D) and I agreed a deal and boy oh boy what a great party it was. The venue was the Two Brewers, just off Jamaica road, and very close to the Thames, owned by Arthur, this was Bermondsey old school, more shootings in this pub than Dodge city.

The food was laid out gloriously on a group of trestle tables adorned with several whole Salmon, giant Mediterranean prawns, dozens of oysters, this buffet was not from Iceland's. Stevie Supples was a fantastic chef and caterer, and this had all the gastronomical hallmarks of his work. The guests arrived around 7pm, beautiful women and smartly dressed men, the serious drinking got underway, all the party tunes were filling the room "forever in blue jeans" "sweet Caroline" the place was rocking, I remember Julie, who went to St Michaels with me came up and sung "Never been to me" by an artiste called Charlene and the place went "chicken oriental". I did the countdown at midnight and wallop! It was the year 2000! "Happy new year everyone" I shouted down the mic, auld lang syne was played as the guests linked arms, afterwards some of the guests went outside to enjoy the brilliant firework display at Tower bridge, they had a perfect view from just outside the pub, as it lit up the Bermondsey night sky, we partied all night long, there must have been some serious hangovers, but we continued again the following afternoon on New Year's Day in the same pub, that was one hell of a party.

As I reflect on these golden times, there are so many other great parties I have been lucky to play music at, every party gets my same attention, I look at people's body language at my gigs, if they are tapping their toes, singing along, gyrating their hips, I zoom in and go for the jugular. What I mean is, if they are reacting to a certain style of music I will pursue that same musical genre, and I am relentless in my pursuit of them enjoying themselves, that is my aim, my goal. Always be the best that you can be, and they will always dance, all night long.

A tip if you have booked a DJ for your special event. Keep communicating with him/her, make sure they are well watered and had some food off the buffet, they will feel appreciated, never take them for granted. I have been at some gigs where not even a glass of water has been offered or a sausage roll from the buffet. I will never forget a gig I did over the city of London, got there at 3pm finished playing music at midnight, the pub was packed. The guvnor of the pub gave me a ham sandwich! Yes, a ham sandwich, that was my wages! I won't say who it was, as I am not like that, but it's the first gig I have ever done where I left to drive home unpaid, hungry, and skint. On the other end of the scale, I have had plates brimming with grub handed to me, and hundreds of pounds in tips. The point I am making is DON'T FORGET THE DJ, they will give you everything, if you remember that they are there. In a recent gig at the Surdoc club I charged the host a few hundred and at the end of the night he gave me a monkey, I would have been just as happy with a cockle tip and a couple of prawn vol-au-vonts.

Chapter six

PARTY'S AT THE COMMONS

Long before our former Prime minister Boris Johnson started having illegal parties on the parliamentary estate, I am pleased to say, I am the one who started the ball rolling, my parties were organised and legal, and even though I say so myself, they were awesome.

I started working for the Vote office on the parliamentary estate in November 2000 and it was the start of twenty years' service for them. George Archer got me the job and it was taken over by another company in 2012, who messed it up for everyone. The Vote office provided the printed material that was essential for the members of parliament to carry out their jobs. I would help keep the Vote offices stocked with Hansards, budget documents, reports, and many other important publications. I had an impeccable attendance record and was never late for work, that has always been my work ethic, and always will be.

I am not a name dropper but I have shared the House of commons lifts with Margaret Thatcher (very frail) John Major, Tony Blair, Gordon Brown (who was very nice to chat with) Theresa May, David Cameron, and of course Boris Johnson, these meetings in the many lifts on the estate could only take place when they were not Prime minister, as they would have been surrounded by security and I wouldn't be allowed in the lift, so they were either on the way up or on the way down in their political career's respectively. In Margaret Thatcher's case she was old and frail and just about to pop her clogs. I have seen many celebrities that have visited Portcullis house, Noel Edmunds, Jose Mourinho, Hugh Grant, Brian May, Garth Crookes, Yuri Gellar, and

Michael Jackson. Although M.J was from a considerable distance and being followed by a very large entourage.

When I was at school I never thought I would be working at the House of Commons on my 40th birthday but yes a few months after joining the Vote office team I was in the Sports and social club, one of around seventeen bars on the estate and all subsidised, so they were all cheap as chips, when I first started, there was a very strong booze culture amongst the staff and many alcoholics, so I invited a few of my new work colleagues to have a drink with me after work. It was my 40th birthday, It was very uneventful, and I seemed to be the only one buying drinks. The nicest fellow in the Vote office was Owen Sweeney, he bought me a drink and he was one of the bosses. I must admit people that are careful with their money are not my favourite kind of people, especially as we were in a very cheap bar anyway, imagine if we were drinking in the west end, holy shit, I'd die of thirst. My friends in the Commons print services were as good as gold and we would have some great nights with fun and laughter and loads to drink, Monk, Hugh, Frosty, and not forgetting Tom and Paddy, who worked for the vote office, and were all diamond geezers. Fatima in the vote office was my good friend and Sumble was also fun to talk to, we all got on so well.

My daily routine I would get in for 8am, do a couple of hours and have breakfast in the Lord's restaurant then more work till midday and lunch. Afterwards more work till 3pm, have a small break and crack on till home time at 4pm. It was wonderful working in such a prestigious and iconic place, walking under the Big Ben tower several times a day, and passing many familiar members of parliament in the corridors of power.

Our first Christmas party was held at 7 Millbank, and I gained permission from the lovely Jo Pitt who was second in charge of the vote office. I designed the posters and the tickets and with the help of the print unit we printed the tickets and sold them for £5 each, this would pay for the food from Marks and Spencer's and the booze from Sainsburys in Vauxhall. We sold over 200 tickets and with the help of my side kick David Martin, we pulled it off and the annual Christmas party was born. David Martin was a great help in organising these parties, Norman helped too, and I thank them for their help in making it a great success.

The first Christmas party was a great success, there was a lot of drunk people and a lot of flirting with work colleagues, I was a little worse for wear so collected my DJ equipment with my van in the morning. As I walked around the parliamentary estate that day there was some sore heads, but lots of compliments, and Jo Pitt loved it, so it cemented next year's Christmas party, and it was already being planned. Thanks to Mr John Collins who was the deliverer of the vote at the time and joined in all the fun at these special events.

I was asked by Bermondsey beat to play music in between the acts at the Bermondsey carnival known as "The Event". It would take place at Southwark Park in the first week of July and the headliners were Chas & Dave, yes please, I'll have some of that, little did I know Phil Burkett and Russell Dryden would ask me to do this annually for a few years, I was well chuffed. I have to say a massive thank you to Bermondsey Beat for asking me to DJ at the "Event" I will always be grateful, and I miss it very much, but all good things come to an end.

On the day I arrived at 10am and set up my sound equipment with the p.a. providers and waited for the first act, they were due on at 12 noon and after a sound check they dually obliged. The Bermondsey carnival was underway. This is where the carnival should always take place, in later years it had to move to "The Bandstand", but right now we had well over 5,000 music lovers in the park waiting for the main act. My job was to warm the crowd up before the main act would take to the stage in just under an hours' time.

I had the crowd by the short and curlies, they were in the palm of my hand, and I loved them singing back to me to "Sweet Caroline" and "Rocking all over the world", I felt so comfortable, this is what I was meant to do, the buzz was incredible, I did what was asked of me and more. Russell from Bermondsey beat took the mic and thanked everyone for coming, and calmly announced "Ladies and gentlemen, please welcome to the event Southwark Park, Chas & Dave!". The crowd went crazy, and Chas & Dave smashed it. I was lucky enough to work with Chas and Dave a few times privately, and when I heard that Chas Hodges had died, it was very sad news, and I for one was gutted, and I knew then, they would never play Southwark Park again.

The next Vote office Christmas party was well organised and proved more popular than the first one, again it was in 7 Millbank, but this time we had barmaids, and loads of ice to cool the tins of grog. The place was rocking and packed to the rafters, it was time to get a bigger venue I thought, it was great to see all the commons staff dancing to the sounds of Amy Winehouse and Candi Staton, another good day at the office, roll on next year, I have a great idea, it's time for the Christmas boat party!

Another year at the Bermondsey Carnival our headliner was "The Blockheads", obviously, the remains of Ian Dury's band, these musicians were so tight, they were brilliant, they opened their set with "Reasons to be cheerful Part three" and carried out a ninety minute set that was musically brilliant, all sections of the band were spot on, the percussion and the saxophonist being my favourite, "Hit me with your rhythm stick" ending the show to a great ovation. What an honour for me, to play music before they took the stage, such a brilliant band.

Apart from tight fisted people, other types get right on my nerves, people on Facebook that show pictures of food that they are about to eat! Is it in case they get food poisoning? I have seen pictures of pie n mash!! Come on its not even very pretty on a plate. And the ones that write something like this "God rest her soul; she has been taken far too soon" I want to know who they are talking about; it is so infuriating. When I die, please just say it how it is "Noel's dead!" there, you have my permission.

I love traveling and have been to many places around the world, I really want to get back to the Top3 bar in Rhodes, it has so many cool memories for me.

I had a great time in Las Vegas, I stayed at Caesars Palace in an executive suite, I had my own state room within my room, a double bed, giant screen and a jacuzzi the size of a small swimming pool. This was the weekend of Hurricane Katrina that devastated New Orleans in August 2005, it was very hot in Vegas, thank God for air conditioning. When I walked outside the hotel to go to the hotel across the street for something to eat, the heat would hit you like you were walking into an oven, once inside the hotel on the other side it was cool again like a fridge. While I was there, I went on a helicopter ride to the Grand Canyon, over the hoover dam and a view from the sky of Celine Dion's home. We landed in a gauge with the the river flowing a long way below where we stood. The pilot retrieved a hamper from the helicopter, and we all had a champagne breakfast in the heat of the morning sun. On the way back we set down again and refuelled and set off again as we flew down the famous Vegas strip.

That night I was in the third row for Celine Dion at Caesars and Hollywood great Debbie Reynolds was sitting in the front row with, what looked like her grandchildren, I could have reached out and touched them, but I sat back and enjoyed the show, Celine Dion is not really my bag, but when in Vegas. She was very good actually. I also went to Paris Paris hotel to watch Ben Elton's "We will rock you" featuring the music of rock band Queen. My final show was at the Mandalay Bay hotel, right near the airport, the hotel had its own man-made beach with a massive wave machine. It was here I saw one of the last ever concerts of "Destiny's child", not long after this gig they split, but hey what a concert, Beyonce can sing but boy she can move her booty too.

The next House of Commons Christmas party was going to be onboard the Pride of London riverboat, my friend Steven Woollacott owns the boat, and has worked all his life on the river. Tickets went on sale for £10 and we sold out very quickly, 200 tickets gone in a flash, we had 3 deejays DJ Nik Nak, DJ Frosty, and Bermondsey's number one!! We were all looking forward to the challenge of playing to all the parliamentary staff, Sparky's, Chippy's, Cooks, Cleaners, all sorts of professions.

We boarded at Westminster pier at 6pm, Nik and Frosty opened with some great tunes as people got familiar with the boat, very soon the upper deck was bouncing with people dancing all over the deck. By the time I started playing there was some very drunk people about, all the Christmas favourites "Last Christmas" "The Fairy-tale of New York" "All I want for Christmas is you", as the riverboat passed under Tower bridge there was a terrific atmosphere, after four hours of pulsating music and the sights of London town we dis-embarked at Westminster pier, inebriated and with sore feet. All for just a tenner. Merry Christmas everyone.

The Bermondsey Carnival "The Event" Southwark Park was ready to go again, this time with Nine below zero and top of the bill, Bill Wyman's Rhythm Kings, these two bands were awesome, and it was an honour to play on the same stage as Bill Wyman, an original member of the Rolling Stones! He spoke to me! He said, "you got a light mate?" quickly I said, "I don't smoke Bill" and he wondered off looking to light his cigarette, as far as I was concerned, it was a conversation with a rock n roll legend. Apart from Bill, Andy Fairweather Lowe was in the band, who had a big hit with "Wide eyed and legless" and was a member of a successful Welsh band "Amen Corner", who had a number one hit with (If paradise) is half as nice. Grammy award winner Albert Lee was also in the band and featured with a fantastic ten-minute guitar solo, this band was one of the best I had seen, and they completely smashed it. If ever I win the national lottery, I have dreamt this scenario a million times, I would put on a free show in Southwark Park featuring the music of Squeeze, Madness, and a few Soul giants, make it a day to remember, but I do need to win a fortune first.

Nine below zero had appeared for Bermondsey beat several times before, they are still touring Europe, and are a very popular blues band, they played a very tight ninety-minute set, I am sure they will play again at the "Event" very soon. It is quite incredible for me to play music before these acts take to the stage, and in front of so many music fans, this year's Bermondsey carnival was cancelled due to lack of funds, we can't let the council get away with this, the Bermondsey community look forward to this each summer, if they get away with it once, they will try and get away with it next year.

I left the House of Commons in 2019 and still have some great friends there, Frosty, Hugh, Monk, Tom, Fatima, they all keep in touch and are all very nice people. I enjoyed my time there; it was an experience believe me, I was there when the police officer was killed at the gates of parliament, and another time when a car driver tried to ram the barriers. Scary times, I know I did the best I could, but like politics, nothing is forever, even your job.

Thanks to Colin James, who came to the rescue and offered me a job delivering Patisserie in the west-end, unfortunately lots of work for very little money, but it helped me out at the time, and I was grateful for the work. Getting to London's famous flower market Covent Garden early in the morning and walking into a fridge first thing, certainly woke me up It didn't last long, I couldn't do Saturday's, so I had to make a choice, sticky toffee pudding or playing music down the Gordon Arms, music always wins! Thank you, Colin, much appreciated.

Next job was delivering stationary to the city of London in the early hours of the morning, although when I started, I was delivering the same stuff down the A13 to Southend and the surrounding areas. I have to say, Essex people are really nice, bit like Bermondsey folk, except we are on one side of the river, and they are on the other. I much preferred working in the early hours, no traffic, no wardens, it was just very easy, I would be home by six am. I would be delivering to Banks and solicitors who preferred deliveries in the early hours, they realised the traffic and parking difficulties, and their loading bays were always manned.

In March 2020 this job, like many others finished because of lockdown. Little did I know my next job would be the best job I could ever imagine, because Bermondsey radio was born, and all will be revealed later in the second half of the book.

CHAPTER SEVEN

The Ashes in Australia and the Olympic games in Athens

2005 and England won the Ashes 2-1, in England, and I made up my mind, I am off to Oz, and this was going to be my best holiday ever, and it was. November 2006, I set off to Melbourne Australia from London Heathrow via Singapore with Qantas, I couldn't sleep on the twenty-four-hour flight, I was so excited, I booked it all myself, internal flights, accommodation, concerts and two test matches at Brisbane and Adelaide. When I arrived in Oz, I went straight to my hotel in Bourke Street in the centre of Melbourne, it was 1am, I left my cases in my room and found a bar open and had a few drinks I thought I was the only Englishman in Australia, but the barman was from Camberwell. I would find out there was thousands of Brits in Australia and after a few large scotches I gave up the fight to stay awake and retired wearily to my room, I was out for the count, and woke at 2pm in the afternoon totally jet lagged. I went out and got lunch, the food in Oz is so nice and good value, I had a nice fillet steak, mushrooms, and peas. Washed down by a schooner of beer. I went back to my room to get ready for my first concert on my itinerary, I was off to the Rod Laver arena to see Carole King. I took a taxi to the arena and made my way inside and naturally got a beer, I had a look round, it was a very modern complex, it is the place where the Australian open takes place, and it was easy to get a beverage. I had made an effort, I was wearing a Burberry shirt and a brown pair of Gucci shoes, I looked and felt good and out of the corner of my eye was a nice curvy young lady, and on her own! I didn't mess about, I shuffled over and coolly enquired "hiya, how are you doing?" "I am fine mate" she replied in a local accent and a lovely smile. "Can I get you a drink?" I asked "Yes please, that's very nice of you, I'll have a gin and tonic" she said, I think I've pulled, I thought. We had a great conversation, she was from Brisbane her name was Shaz, and she had flown in for the concert, she had a seat in another section of the arena, so I asked if she wanted to go out after the concert for drinks, holy shit, she said yes! We agreed to meet near the bar we had been drinking at, and low and behold, there she was, after a great concert by Carole King, waiting for me, bloody hell this pulling game is easy. We jumped in a cab and headed for downtown Melbourne and the talkative driver recommended an Irish bar, and he subsequently dropped us outside it. Once inside, lots of singing and dancing, and plenty of Guinness. I was a bit pissed and was still getting used to the time difference, She insisted that she walked me to my hotel on Bourke street, she was concerned I might get lost on my first proper night in Oz, at the reception of the hotel we kissed and I invited her in for a night-cap, but she politely declined, instead she gave me her number in Brisbane and suggested I rang her when I arrived there a few days later, I never did call her, unfortunately I lost her number in transit, I was gutted, you see, I don't always get me leg over!

Next day in Melbourne I had a ticket for the Telstra dome, to see Irish rock band U2.

I woke up with a bit of a hangover and disappointed that Shaz didn't come up for a "Night-cap", we had a great night, and what an introduction to the Aussie nightlife. I got myself organised and set off looking for a café for some breakfast. It's very hilly Melbourne, with tramlines throughout, but I just kept on walking until I found a greasy spoon. It was worth the trek, two eggs, bacon, sausages, mushrooms, two slices, and a large mug of coffee, absolutely handsome! It was called the Bubble café and was owned by a Greek family, and we all know the cockney slang for Greeks....yes Bubble and squeak.

Kanye West opened for U2 at the Telstra dome, he went down very well singing "Gold digger" and "Stronger" I had a thirst on and was downing a pint or two before U2 came on stage, I was chatting to two girls from Rochdale who were working in Oz, they were living the dream, I was very envious. U2 didn't disappoint, hit after hit, I just wished Bono would keep out of politics, drives me nuts, apart from that they were brilliant as usual, the first time I saw them live was at Wembley at the famous "Live Aid" concert, these days they are so much more visual, with giant screens all-round the stage. Superb sound. It's the politics that does my head in.

Next day and I had a flight to catch to Sydney, better have an early night, my sleeping pattern is still a bit messed up, looking forward to my next flight, less than two hours over the blue mountains and Sydney opera house and bosh I'll be there. I flew with Jet Star and the aircraft had leather seats throughout, and plenty of leg room. The flight was very cheap too, all my internal flights are with Jet Star, happy days.

Sydney is a fantastic city and they put on the best New Year's Eve firework display in the world, it goes on for thirty minutes and synchronised with an awesome soundtrack. I was staying in Manly, in a massive apartment just a few steps from the sandy beach, Manly is just a short ferry trip from the centre of Sydney. It is also where they film for a tv series called "Home and away". During my stay in Manly I discovered the best fish and chip shop, everything was cooked to order, and the wet fish was on display for you to pick the one that took your fancy. I had a great day on the beach and decided to get Fish and chips on the way back to my apartment. The fish was so nice, and such large portions of both the fish and the crispy brown chips, After the meal I fell into a deep sleep and woke early the next morning feeling fresh and regenerated.

No concerts for me in Sydney so I thought I must explore this brilliant city, I didn't fancy walking across the Sydney harbour bridge, so I set off for Bondi beach on the other side of the harbour. I got a bus there and, I must admit, I felt a bit awkward putting my England flag towel on the beach next to a couple of "Sheila's". It's a nice beach, don't get me wrong, but I was expecting something more spectacular. I spent a couple of hours there and got a bit bored, so I made my way to the city centre. I went up the Sydney tower and got excellent views of the harbour and the city skyscrapers, did a bit of shopping, bought a couple of T-shirts, and hopped on the Manly ferry and thought to myself, I think I'll have an early night, and I did.

Next morning I was off to Brisbane, where I had arranged to meet up with a former work colleague from the House of Commons, Rob was waiting for me at the airport and after dropping off my luggage at the hotel we went out on the lash in Brisbane town centre, Rob, who is Australian had married his wife Erica in England, they decided that the best choice for them was Australia, and they were right, as they are still there today, just outside Brisbane. It was great to see Rob again and chat about the good old days at the Vote office.

The next day 23rd November I put on my white England cricket shirt, nice and early, and tucked into a large breakfast in the hotel's restaurant. This morning I was heading for the "Gabba" for the first test of the Ashes series. Wow Bermondsey's number one DJ was 12,000 miles from home, and about to watch England defend the urn, is this for real? Am I dreaming?

Steve Harmison ran in with the first delivery, and it was the widest wide I'd ever seen! The Aussies cheered sarcastically, and that one ball summed up the tour, we lost the match, and we lost the series and the ashes 5-0.

The next two nights I went to see two colossal music stars at the same venue, but on separate nights, first up it was Elton John, it was a terrible show, I had seen him many times before in England and he was normally very good, but He started with "Philadelphia freedom" and "Benny and the Jets" all good. Then he said disappointingly "I'm now going to do a few songs off of the new album". Oh my God, after the fifth new track in a row, people started to walk out! Then suddenly Elton, mid song got off his stool and hastily walked off stage, his band continued with an extended instrumental version of the song! Ten minutes later Elton returned, apparently, he had been sick at the side of the stage, but like a true professional he carried on, and to be fair he recovered the show too, although at this point the arena was half empty. "Come on Elton I've travelled 12,000 miles to see this shit!" I felt like saying, but I kept my mouth shut, and staggered back to my hotel, slightly worse for wear thinking, I got to do this all again tomorrow. And the second day of the test match!

On the way back to Brisbane central the train was quite packed, but somehow an Aussie drunk found me! He offered me a drink from his can of special brew, when I said, "No thanks, I'm fine mate" he looked at me suspiciously as he listened to my accented reply "It's a bloody Limey!" He shouted, the rest of the carriage laughed, I blushed and smiled at the same time thinking "Pisshead!" Here was me, a right piss head, calling a down and out aboriginal bloke a pisshead, very rich from me, considering I could hardly stand up straight myself.

After another hot day at the "Gabba" and England wasn't doing very well in the field, I remember being shocked by the language of the Australian fans directed towards Ashley Giles, who was fielding on the boundary "Ashley Giles you're a c**t!" I was gobsmacked, and Giles just looked embarrassed. I left early to get ready for the nights action. A bit of grub and I was on my way to the Brisbane arena for part two of the entertainment, surely Billy Joel was going to put on a great show, wasn't he? I can only describe the two shows as chalk and cheese, it was one of the best shows I have ever seen in my life! The music, the band, the showman, that is Billy Joel. The crowd was into it right from the very beginning, and it didn't fade, and we all knew the songs, every single one of them, I will just say that when Billy sang "Piano Man" they could hear the crowd singing the chorus in Brisbane city centre, FANTASTIC! I was relatively sober as I made my way back to my hotel, didn't see my Aussie pal, thank God. It was a great night though, if you get the chance go see Billy Joel, you will love it.

I liked Brisbane, it was at the end of November, and it was very hot, and next to the casino there was a large Christmas tree, and it would light up at night flashing its coloured bulbs, and I was standing there in just a t-shirt and shorts in the heat of the night, it was weird, but I was in Australia after all.

Next day I prepared myself for another train journey, this time it would be a twenty-four-hour trip up the east coast of Australia, Brisbane to Cairns, the anticipation as I stood on the platform waiting for the bullet like train to pull into the station was very exciting, and it didn't disappoint. I guess this was a bit like travelling on the orient express but Aussie style. The porters wouldn't let me leave my suitcase at the drop off point, it was 27kgs, too heavy apparently, so I carried it on the train myself. It was a very long modern sky-blue train, very sleek, and inside the seats were spacious and comfy. While we were waiting for the clock to come round to the top of the hour the train driver let me in the driver's cab, full of dials and levers and with a big glass screen. I returned to my reserved seat and the train left around 7pm and smoothly gathered speed, knowing that the same time next day it would be arriving in the tropical city of Cairns. I went to the buffet car and met some interesting passengers with fascinating tales to tell, I had one or two to tell them. Several beers later many stories told,

I bid my new friend's good night and retired to my seat and the train gently rocked me to sleep.

The journey was sublime, in the morning looking out the window of the train and watching the world glide by as it made its way to Cairns. A few stops along the way and soon the tropical fields of bananas came into view, indicating that we were getting close. The carriage I was in was relatively empty and at the next stop an aboriginal man got on and sat on the other side of the carriage, in just flip flops, shorts and a sleeveless shirt, within minutes of leaving the station the ticket inspector walked through the train and asked me for my ticket. I showed him mine, and satisfied, he looked at the man in the flip flops and shook his head, knowing full well he wasn't going to have one. He just carried on through the train, he didn't need the hassle. 7pm and we arrived at Cairns, and I jumped in the hotel's courtesy bus direct to my hotel, checked in, and went to the bar for a few beers, as you do.

In the morning I had a nice breakfast and got ready for my trip. I had booked an excursion to Green Island; this place was on the great barrier reef, and I was looking forward to it very much indeed. I got a taxi down to the harbour and found my tour boat moored very near to where the taxi had dropped me off. Around fifty tourists boarded the vessel and off we set for Green Island. This trip took about forty-five minutes, the sea was a bit choppy, and the sun was high in the sky and very hot. On arrival we all swapped boats and I boarded a large glass bottomed boat, this was an excellent experience, and as we moved away from the sandy beach more and more colourful fish came into view, it was like being inside a large fish tank and the giant angel fish coloured blue, green, yellow, and swimming all-round the boat. It was fantastic to see the reef so close and personal. The fish were attracted to the boat by food thrown into the sea by the crew, and the tourists were delighted by the tropical fish turning up in large shoals, as if by magic. After taking a few pictures the boat headed back to the pier. Soon after

I went to the crocodile sanctuary, I was first visitor of the morning and I bumped into one of the Keepers and we had a chat while I was observing a pond surrounded by a fence that was six feet tall. It looked like a stagnant pool to me, I enquired "Is there nothing in there?" pointing at the stagnant pool. The keeper had a stick in his hand and replied "Oh yes, there is something in their mate" he took his stick and poked it in between the gap in the 6-foot-high fence. He very gently touched the surface of the pool, and Whooooosh!! a giant croc jumped from the water, swishing its tail! thank God for the fence!!, It splashed down into the pool soaking me in the process, and immediately submerged, leaving just its eyes and nostrils above the surface, seconds later it had disappeared under the dirty water, and once again I was convinced there was nothing in the stagnant pool. The keeper looked at me shook his head and laughed and said "You pomms, You pomms". How was I supposed to know there was a crocodile in there? Apparently, I read later the crocodile has a strategy of lying still for hours, conserving its energy, and when prey comes along it pounces! Next day I was booked to go into the rain forest via cable car and it was another great experience in Cairns, I loved it, it was about forty-five minutes until I reached the top, the views were amazing, and after viewing the lush vegetation, Keith our tour guide warned us to avoid all the creepy Crawley's, including the deadly spiders and venomous snakes, that are lurking in the undergrowth. Cheers Keith, I am not going into the undergrowth thanks very much, I will stay on the paths. I noticed our steam train, that would take us back down to sea level wasn't leaving for ninety minutes, I already had my ticket, so I noticed just across the road was a Pub! Time for a drink.

Inside the pub I was joined by a young Irish lady, that was living and working in Cairns, she was from the same town in Ireland where my family were from, a place called Blanchardstown, in the outskirts of Dublin, what are the chances of that? We got on very well indeed, and when it was time for me to go, we arranged to meet in the Irish pub in the centre of town later that evening. I was there, but she walked past, I saw her, maybe she was meeting me at another Irish pub, but I didn't follow her, I didn't want to end up in the slammer like Ned Kelly. I sat there and finished my pint of Australian Guinness. Arhhh it was lovely.

I had a flight next day, but I couldn't resist the swimming pool back at the hotel, it was decorated like a lagoon and before retiring to my room I had a nice swim. Soon I dried myself down and headed to my room and crashed out. I got a lift to Cairn's airport in the hotel shuttle bus, It was a three-and-a-half-hour flight to Adelaide and upon arrival got a taxi to my motel "The flying Scotsman". It had a massive kilted Scottish guardsman very visible from the road, it was a very comfortable motel. There was a pub across the road that had pokies along the bar, "Pokies" were gambling machines, and this pub had a betting shop within It, not forgetting an off license at the side of the pub. I Had a few Schooners in there on that first night in Adelaide, very friendly folk. I didn't feel 12,000 miles from home, they made me very welcome.

1st December. In the morning it was time for Test match number two. It was a twenty-minute bus ride into the city centre and the Adelaide Oval, what a magnificent ground, it had a statue of one of the greatest batsmen of all time, Donald Bradman outside. England got off to a great start, they batted first and put-up a sizable first innings total 551/6 Declared with the help of Kevin Pietersen (158) and Paul Collingwood (206), unfortunately the Aussies had Ricky Pontin!

I had a date that night so at the end of the days play I quickly got back for a shit, shower, and a shave at my motel, and smartened myself up and headed back into the centre of Adelaide. I had been chatting with Joanne in a chat group called Adelaide chat, and we agreed to meet up when I visited, she was 32 and divorced with two small kids, just a few days ago we chatted from the other side of the world, and here we were sitting in a restaurant having a meal together, it is bonkers, and the crazy thing was, that we actually fancied each other! She had a lovely personality and a wicked smile, and we immediately hit it off. We had a lovely meal and a couple of beers and decided to head back to the motel via the off licence to grab a couple of bottles of chilled wine. Back at the motel mine and Joanne's clothes came off quickly, and we ended up having lots of fun for a few hours and, both exhausted, fell asleep in each other's arms. She left in the morning and we lost touch, but she was a lovely lady and she made it a very special night. That morning I was getting ready for more cricket, it was a bit chilly, but I insisted on wearing just a t-shirt and shorts, big mistake, a fresh wind was blowing across the ground and although it was sunny it was cold, which is unusual for Adelaide. That night, and I don't know why I bought a ticket, I went to see Kylie at the Adelaide arena, it was ok, but I left early, and it took me ages to get a cab and head back to my motel, I polished off the wine in the fridge, that was left over from the night before. Next day I flew back to Melbourne and got a cab to the same hotel that I stayed in when I arrived, on Bourke Street. That day I did last minute shopping, I was flying back to London the following day and was looking for last minute bargains. I ended up in a sports bar watching the cricket that I had just recently attended, a few hundred miles away.

What a fantastic holiday I had, met some wonderful people, experienced the Australian culture, the food, the sun, and the Sheila's, and I have to say, if I ever won a fortune on the lottery, this is the place I'd come, it is by far the best place I have ever been, I promise you.

When I boarded the Qantas jet for home, I was not looking forward to the long flight to London Heathrow via Hong Kong, as I fastened the seat belt the captain came across the intercom and welcomed us all on the flight and added "Just some breaking news, Australia have won the second test at Adelaide beating England to go 2-0 up in the series" a big cheer went out throughout the aircraft, (not from me) that's the Australian sense of humour for you, I didn't find it a bit funny, Basterd.

The Charcoal burner was a pub in Sidcup Road and the owner was Stan Smith, looked a little bit like Dudley Moore, and a lovely guy. It was coming up to May bank holiday and he booked me in to do the Sunday before the Monday, so nobody had to go to work the next day. What followed was an amazing Sunday, packed with people from all over the manor. They had a barbecue outside and loads of bar staff, Stan told me later that he took £10,000 on that Sunday, and he wouldn't take that sort of money all week! Bermondsey's number one was packing them in!

Word spreads quickly in Sidcup/Eltham and on Tuesday I get a call from the guvnor of The Beehive pub, near New Eltham train station. She said "I would like you to work here every Saturday night for the forceable future, if you're interested" I told her I would get back to her the next day with my decision. It was a yes, and I started the following weekend. It just shows you how competitive it is down that way. They loved the music I played, and they were determined to have me in the pub most Saturday nights.

Let me tell you, this pub was a nuthouse! I thought the Lill was a crazy gaff, but The Beehive took the biscuit. I think there must have been a nutty asylum nearby because I saw some fruit and nutcases on the dance floor, I've never seen people dance like that before. Period.

Joking aside, this place was full of beautiful girls, all dressed so fine, and up for a party, and I gave it to them every Saturday night for two years. I set up the full four speaker sound system and all the latest lighting, then they had my experience and extensive record collection. While I was in there playing music guvnors of other pubs sent people in there to try and persuade me to work for their pub, yes it was very competitive round that neck of the woods.

The Beaverwood club – Chislehurst, was one of those places that approached me at the time, and I duly accepted, every second Friday playing soul/Motown and party tunes in a nice club in Chislehurst. Lovely people, great dancing, and very warm atmosphere. We had to move to the Birchwood golf club because of redevelopment of the Beaverwood, but the new venue was better for facilities and accessibility and the same crowd followed her to the new place. Unfortunately, she passed away soon after, and we closed it down. It was a shame because it was proving very popular.

The Gordon arms – Chislehurst, was a great pub, run by the beautiful Mandy, I would appear there every month or so, always packed with nice people as customers. I was reacquainted with Mandy's mum Lill, who worked as a bar maid for Albert Lawson in the Swan and Sugarloaf, we would play some great soul classics in the Gordon's, and we had a few fantastic New Year's Eve party's as well. They spent a few quid on that boozer looked very smart in the end. Then the bombshell, the owner got rid of Mandy, to everyone's surprise, and I haven't worked there since. In honour of a great guvnor, we had a special leaving party at the Bull's head in Chislehurst for Mandy and so many regulars turned up, to wish her all the best.

If there is one thing I can't stand its Karaoke, they ask me if they can sing a song and I say "I am sorry but the mic is for my voice only, and not for people trying to sing" they always turn away disappointed, but in all the years they have succeeded in getting their hands on my mic, I have never heard a good voice, just people shouting, out of time, and very pitchy. These pitchy singers, think they are good, and I can tell you for a fact, they are not. It's got to a stage now, where I must leave a pub if Karaoke starts, my ears can't take it anymore. I wish someone would tape it and play it back to them in the cold light of day, they sound so bad.

Proud to say I have helped raise thousands of pounds for various charities, on Bermondsey radio we have an appeal at the moment to help children of Bermondsey receive a Christmas present on Christmas day, these children are less fortunate than most, we collected over 100 presents last year, this year all donations that you donate to Bermondsey radio will all go to our "Toy Drive" please help if you can this Christmas and thank you. In the past I have had the honour to play music at many fundraisers including for Bermondsey superhero Kevin Downey, who has raised over one hundred thousand pounds for various causes over the years, running the London Marathon many times, this man deserves a special community award for his endless steps in the fight against cancer and other great causes.

August 2004, I was off to Athens for the summer Olympic games, I always wanted to experience it, and where better, than the place it started. I flew out on an easy jet flight to Athens and believe it or not sitting in front of me was newsreader Natasha Kaplinsky, and I thought, easyJet? no way. She is worth a fortune and should be flying British airways surely. Anyhow we arrived on Saturday morning and team GB were rowing their way to gold medals, this was the time of Steve Redgrave and Mathew Pinsent, soon the medals were piling in, and it proved a very successful games for our team. I stayed just outside the centre of Athens with family of Spiro, the owner of the "Top three Bar" in Rhodes, they were so good to me, a lovely family and all the hotels in Athens were booked-up, and very expensive. I went to see the beach volley ball, the trap shooting and rifle events, but most of my tickets were inside the Olympic stadium morning and evening sessions, During the morning sessions I would be in the company of the family of British decathlete Dean Macey, who after a terrific effort finished fourth and just out of the medals, I remember commiserating with Dean's father after the placings were confirmed and telling him "your son did us proud".

I was in the Olympic stadium in the evening's when the 100 metres final was run, Justin Gatlin winning the gold in 9.85 seconds, and I was lucky enough to see Dame Kelly Holmes win gold in the 800 metres and on the same night she received her medal from Lord Coe. Standing for the national anthem with the rest of the crowd and singing "God save the Queen" was one of proudest moments of my life, as the union flag is raised tears ran down my cheek and I was there! It was fantastic, very emotional. Dame Kelly went on to win the 1500 metres too, a double gold Olympic dream. I also saw a world record in the lady's pole vault by Yelena Isinbeyava with a height of 4.91 metres, what a feeling to see a world record, even though she was a Russian.

I was there when Manchester United won the Treble in 1999, at the Nou Camp, the home of Barcelona, we were playing the German side Bayern Munich, and to be honest we didn't play very well, we were without the injured Paul Scholes, and the suspended Roy Keane, so it was always going to be a tough match. I travelled with the London Supporters branch of MUFC, Ralph Mortimer was top man of the branch and provided us all with tickets for the game, we stayed in Lloret de Mar, in a hotel way above the beach. At the Nou Camp, we were positioned behind the goal where all three goals went in, and what a great atmosphere in the stadium, even better after the final whistle.

We met at Semley place, just behind Victoria coach station, that is where we met for all games that was traveling out of London, including games at Old Trafford, this time when we met, it was with suitcases, a twenty-four-hour coach ride to Lloret de mar, Costa brava, Spain. This would leave us a 30 minutes' drive to the stadium. Our hotel was on top of the cliff above the beach and after we had won the cup and eventually got back to our rooms, we could see the Germans had set fire to the stacks of deck chairs on the beach below (bad losers). I have to say that was one hell of a coach journey, no amount of pit stops could cushion the blow, and I was thinking with two minutes left in the

European cup final, and the Germans one-up and already lighting flares and celebrating "What the fuck did I do all that traveling for?".
Suddenly there was a corner for United and I could see Schmeichel, our goalkeeper running up field to join his teammates in the box, the corner came in, there was panic in the penalty area and wallop! Teddy Sheringham kicks it into the back of the net! Absolute pandemonium breaks out amongst the United fans, in complete contrast the German players fell to the pitch on their knees and their supporters just couldn't believe it, 1-1 and we're going to extra time! maybe it was worth coming here after all! Just a couple of moments later and the ball was in Bayern's penalty area again, It falls to Ole and wallop, I have just seen Man U win the European cup, I am crying at the final whistle, jumping around screaming with all the other red shirts, my first thought was for my dad in heaven, he was watching too, he was sharing this moment with me, my dad started me following Manchester United when I was a saucepan-lid at just eight years old in 1969, thirty years later 26th May was and always will be the greatest day of my life. Dad thank you for what you did for me, I miss you and Mum so much.

Chapter Eight

TOP VENUES BIG JOBS

When you get a reputation, you must always live up to that expectation, the pressure is always on, its relentless, no standing still, always going forward. If someone see's you for the first time, in the street, in the pub, at a gig, that is what they will think of you forever more. Always be nice, always say hello and never do a bad gig. Those are the rules, and I will always abide by them.

My good friend Jimmy Wood rang me and said his future son in law Joe Little and his daughter were getting married in Italy on Lake Como and they wanted me to DJ at the reception. They would fly me out and put me up in a nice hotel, paying all my expenses. Joe Little worked for Millwall football club as a youth team coach at the time and wanted the best wedding ever, and I think they pulled it off. The logistics of organising such a luxurious wedding is quite a daunting prospect, but it worked. I was set up in a courtyard covered in flowers, and it overlooked Lake Como, you could see the boats passing by and the busy cafés and bars on the other side of the lake, it was stunning. During the meal, I remember I played "The most beautiful girl in the world" by Charlie Rich and announced I was playing this for the beautiful bride, Dionne, and everyone sang along, the song for the first dance was Gladys Knight and the pips, and "You're the best thing that ever happened to me". I have played music at thousands of weddings since 1979, and I have to say there have been lots of great venues, but this one was the best, everything went so brilliantly, and I was looked after very well indeed. The pressure from everyone, the family, and the guests are weighed on your shoulders, and the new bride and groom are counting on you to deliver on their special day. All that expense, and organisation for one day. I was honoured and privileged to be asked, and more important, they trusted me, and I paid them back for that trust.

The following year I did it all over again, but this time the couple hired an island in the centre of the lake and at the end of the night there was a twenty-minute firework display, that was fantastic, and lit up the night sky with all sorts of colours, loud bangs and explosions that ended the reception in style. Lake Como is a wonderful place for a wedding reception, but you must have a few quid in the bank. The married couple had a wedding party for friends and family when they returned to London who couldn't make it to the Italian reception, this venue was very plush and very near Holborn. I think it's called the Rosewood and I was asked to play at this reception too, I must have something over deejays don't have, because once again I went down very well indeed.

Claridge's was another plush venue in the west-end and was a real thrill to play there for another great wedding, it was black tie, and everyone looked splendid, right at the very last minute the organiser said I couldn't bring my sound system into the venue, so she hired a sound and light system from a specialist P.A provider, I just turned up with my laptop and midi controller. What followed was an old school dance fest, with nonstop anthems, dancing everywhere, drinks flowing, and awesome venue.

The Dorchester Hotel on Park Lane is my favourite, such tradition, and so luxurious, I worked here on Christmas day in the same suite Whitney Houston stayed in the last time she came to London. It was for an X Factor appearance, it was painful to watch her on the tv, I don't watch this program normally, it was Whitney though. Simon Cowell has ruined the Christmas number one, and music in general.

Whitney's suite took up most of the 13th floor and I set up and played most of the afternoon and the early part of the evening, I think I stopped around 9.30pm and everyone had a great day, the host came up to me and said "Noel, we have a surprise for you, we got you a room, so you can have a drink and enjoy the night, you don't have to drive home" and gave me a card key for my room. "Wow" I said, "that is unbelievable, thanks very much" This family has a special place in my heart, I will never forget the kindness they have shown me, as long as I live.

I started knocking back the gold watches (scotches) and it turned out to be a very Merry Christmas. It didn't take me long to catch up, they had a head start but I was now knocking back large ones, it wouldn't be long before I was well pickled. A couple of hours later I finally made it back to my room in the Dorchester hotel, a little worse for wear, it was unbelievable, the carpet, the bathroom suite, the TV, the fridge full of booze, hey, this must be your normal life if you're a rock star, why they used to throw tv sets out the window I never know. I got myself ready for bed turned the lights down and put my head on the pillow, it was like resting my head on a cloud, I was asleep in seconds.

In the morning I had a very dry mouth, It was as though I had been licking the Axminster all night. I had a shower and put on the clothes from the day before, my van was already loaded with the sound system and was waiting for me in a side street. I sat on the edge of the bed and reached for the fridge door, a bottle of water was drunk hastily, and I gathered myself together and made my way down to reception. The receptionist was stunning, absolutely gorgeous I handed her my card key and said in my deepest manly voice "I am just checking out, had a bottle of water, my room was paid for by my host, but I owe you for a small bottle of water" The receptionist checked my story and looking up at me she said "Yes sir, a bottle of water, that will be £9.50 please" blimey! Thanks god I didn't have a few gold watches I'd be Dickie Mint! (Skint). I rolled a cockle (ten) from my wad, passed it to her and extravagantly said "Keep the change darlin" I swaggered out to my van very confidently, thinking to myself I have just stayed the night at the Dorchester hotel! I got into my Renault Kangoo and headed back to South-east London, and the Dickens estate, mange tout, mon Cherie, mange tout.

The Carlton tower Jumeirah is situated in Sloane Street, I played here a couple of times, both on a Christmas day. The room was always set out beautifully, with the best cutlery spread nicely on the long dining table, ready for the Christmas lunch that was being prepared down in the kitchen. This hotel has a sister hotel in Dubai, a six-star hotel including a Helipad on the roof, so you know that this place was a top hotel. 3pm and Father Christmas turned up with a sack full of gifts for the kids, just to see their faces, it was a delight to be there, Rudolph and all the other Reindeer were parked up on the roof, I think they were trying their best to avoid the congestion charge. This family always looked after me, and I always looked after them, with fantastic music and they loved to have a sing song too "American Pie" "Forever in blue jeans" "Dance the night away" This was a magical Christmas, and I will never forget these days and their kindness and generosity, thanks for the great times.

Crystals at Wembley stadium was the official venue of the away team and whoever drew that dressing room would get that venue for their supporters to meet and have a drink before the game. It was a massive venue with one very large ground level floor with several bars and one hell of a sound system, Mick Vinciguerra asked me to play music for the Millwall fans in the playoff final against Bradford and I agreed to it. I set up the p.a with the help of the owners and waited for the fans to arrive. Thousands turned up, and I put on all the Millwall favourites, "Let em come" "Wonderwall" "Hey Jude" "Rocking all over the world" and the place was rocking and when I shouted down the mic "come on you lot, no one likes us" they sang it at the top of their voices, it was brilliant, one of my proudest moments, to have a few thousand lions fans in the palm of my hand, it was wonderful. The result of the match was great too, Millwall won 1-0 with a late goal from Steve Morison and they got promoted to the championship.

When I got back to the Blue Anchor pub in Bermondsey a Millwall fan came up to me and said, "you're the guy from Crystals at Wembley aren't you?" I said, "yes that was me" he said, "that was fantastic mate, you were brilliant". That made me very proud, one of my best moments ever. The pressure was on, and I had to deliver, it all worked out, and the owners of the club were so impressed they kept calling me up to help them for FA cup finals, and some of Tottenham's home games while their new ground was being built. I had to play for Liverpool fans once, I hate Liverpool FC, love scousers, but the football team, nah. My worst nightmare would have been West ham, can you imagine me playing "I'm forever blowing bubbles"? no thank you very much. Thank God it never came about.

There was a place on the other side of the Wembley complex, another Indian run place, I think it had Bobby Moore in its name, and they booked me for Aston villa fans for a playoff final and they were a crazy lot, singing along to "Hi Ho Aston villa!" looking back on it, I must have been very brave back then, they could have turned nasty, I guess, but I made it out alive.

I have played many times at the Den, home of the mighty lions, I am a big fan of Millwall, but not a supporter, there is a big difference, a fan follows the scores on the tv and social media, in other words an armchair fan. A supporter pays to go and watch the team through thick and thin, I love their passion and loyalty, it is great to see, and to be in their company when Millwall win.

I played music in the Millwall executive suites for weddings and fundraiser's many times, but Harry's bar more often, Harry's bar is named after Lions legend Harry Cripps, I was lucky enough to see that team, when Millwall played in an all-white kit Alan Dorney, Barry Kitchener, Derek Possee, Alfie Wood, and Bryan King.

I have to tell you about the Millwall kit man Roy Putt, this man is a legend in my eyes, I was going to Ireland for the weekend to see my cousins, aunties and uncles, I was traveling to Lucan in Dublin, to see auntie Josie and uncle Tommy, Auntie Helen and down to Limerick to see my uncle Sean and auntie Mary, not forgetting my cousins Tony, Martin, Mags, Pauline, Paul and all the rest of the gang. Ireland was playing Holland and won 1-0 in the last of the world cup matches, and England played Germany and thrashed them 5-1 in Germany, I had a twenty Euro bet, England, and Ireland to win, it copped 400 euros! straight in the skyrocket, lovely jubbly. Anyhow, Millwall had an Irish international footballer in the camp, David Sadlier, so Roy arranged for two tickets to be left for me to collect at the box office at Lansdowne Road. While we were waiting for the tickets, my cousin Tony and I noticed a few celebrities arriving. Suddenly a blacked-out limousine pulled up right next to us, it was The Edge from the rock band U2, he didn't recognise me! A man came with our tickets and escorted us to our brilliant seats in the main stand. Ireland won 1-0 and my bet copped when England thrashed the Germans later that night. Thank you, Roy, you are a true Millwall legend.

Like most of Bermondsey, I went to Wembley for the playoff against Scunthorpe United, which they lost unfortunately, got back to SE16 and it was mayhem everywhere, Millwall fans fighting almost everywhere, I went into the Jamo on my return to have a few pints, no sooner had I walked inside, a man sitting on a stool just inside the main door holding his new born son in his arms had an empty light ale bottle smashed over his head, with blood pouring over his baby's white woollen blanket. What happened next was pandemonium. I walked out the door I came in. I thought I'll have one more for the frog and popped in to "The Prince of darkness" otherwise known as the Prince of Wales in Scott Lidgett crescent, when my good friend Irene Forsyth

Andina, who is a wonderful lady, owned the pub, it was a wonderful family place, full of nice people, a great place to have a drink. Not on this day, I ordered a pint and sat at the bar just inside the door, on the Scott Lidgett side of the pub, all of a sudden gun shots were being fired into the door I had just walked through, don't know how nobody got hit, the regulars chased the shooter down the street to no avail, I quickly finished my pint of Stella and slipped out the side door, and left them to it.

When I worked at the House of Commons in Westminster, I worked for the Vote office and each Christmas the office in Portcullis house was decorated with lights and tinsel and other festive bangles. Every year we would have a "switch on" of the lights by the very attractive MP Esther McVey, one year she was preparing to do the honours and suddenly she noticed coming through security at Portcullis house was rock legend Brian May from the rock band Queen, he was there because he has been campaigning for the protection of badgers and was there to speak in one of the many committees. Esther nabbed him and he agreed to turn on the Christmas lights. While he was strolling over, I had a Bluetooth speaker behind the desk in the Vote office and quickly linked it to the music library on my android phone, as he walks into the office I play "Bohemian Rhapsody" he turns to me and says, "Good choice of music mate". I am chuffed, just got a complement from a rock legend. Believe it or not he did it again the following year! This time I played "Don't stop me now" and exactly same response from Brian "Great choice of music mate, oh it's you again!" He only recognised me!

The most famous person I ever met took place where La Pont de la tour stands now, along the river, near Shad Thames. He was filming his latest movie called "Give my regards to Broad Street" and it was around 1983. He also shot part of the music video for the song "No more lonely nights" at a pub I worked many times for Johnny Deverson, The Old justice. Have you guessed who I am talking about yet? yes it was Paul McCartney. I was working just round the corner and heard the rumour, so in my lunch hour I went and watched the filming, I was leaning on the river wall, facing Tower bridge, they were filming on my left, and after a few takes, with Toyah Wilcox. The director, who was just in front of me alongside the camera said, "Ok let's have an hours break for lunch" What happened next was unbelievable, Paul McCartney put down his prop, a big music reel that contained the recording of the new album, and walked over to me and said "How's it going kid?" er excuse me are you talking to me Paul? I was shocked but replied with "It's a shame about John" referring to John Lennon, who had been murdered just a few months before. Paul replied" Yeah, there some nutters about" I agreed, and politely asked for an autograph, and gave him an old envelope that I had on me by chance. He signed it and drew a smiley face and handed it back to me. He said, "See you later" and off he went to his Winnebago for a spot of lunch. WOW. Did that just happen?

When I was a young lad I became a big fan of Squeeze, they had several hits in the early eighties, they were one of the first bands that issued their single releases on different coloured vinyl, which was a real novelty back then. I went to see them many times and they were great live. Jools Holland left the band early on, and I remember Paul Carrack had a period in the band and sung the original vocals on the hit "Tempted". Thanks to the Bermondsey carnival I managed to work with Paul Carrack, Glen Tilbrook, and Chris Difford, and in my opinion, this is how I rate them vocally. The best was Carrack, and he went on to sing with Mike and the mechanics, singing main vocals on "Living years" and "Over my shoulder", but his big hit was with a band called Ace, the song was called "How long?" and he absolutely owns that song, a brilliant vocal performance. Glen was brilliant when he appeared at the carnival "Labelled with love" is one of my favourite Squeeze songs, along with "Pulling mussels from a shell" and he performed them well at Southwark Park. As you all know Chris has a husky rough voice and I don't have to tell you "Cool for Cats" is his song, and his voice suits it very well indeed. They all appeared in different years, and at this time Chris and Glen were not speaking to each other, but I am very pleased to say, soon after, they kissed and made up, and reformed Squeeze and are touring the world more than ever.

The Proclaimers opened the Live 8 concert at Murrayfield stadium in July 2005 to an audience of around two billion people! The following Saturday they were headlining "The Event" Southwark Park in front of a few thousand south Londoners, and quite a few Scottish ex pats. The twin brothers, who front the band, were such down to earth lads, very relaxed and chatting to anyone who wanted a quick chat. I had a brief chat with one of them, but don't ask me which one, their twins remember. I wished him well and told him I was the DJ and would play the party songs/sing-a-longs just before his band took the stage, he said, "See you up there" in his deep Scottish accent, and I did, about an hour later, I recall the song I played before they were introduced was, "Sweet Caroline" and it worked perfectly.

They came on stage to a great welcome and launched straight into "500 Miles", this was one of the best performances I'd seen over the park, absolutely smashed it. Lots of Scottish flags being waved throughout the crowd, singing along to all the lyrics, the twins had beads of sweat running down their faces as they finished a very tight set. They began to walk off stage and we had pre organised an encore, my usual trick was to ask the audience if they would like another song? Of course, they all wanted more, and the Proclaimers duly obliged.

Joe Brown is a legend, a great musician and performer and I worked with him at the Bermondsey carnival, if my mum would have been alive, she would have been so proud of me, she used to work in the canteen at television centre in Wood Lane and often prepared meals for Joe and Sam Kidd while they were there recording tv shows. Joe is still performing today, singing songs like "See you in my dreams" he does a great version of the Chas n Dave classic "Ain't no pleasing you" and is a fine musician, he plays Banjo, Mandolin and not forgetting the Ukulele, all, very well indeed.

When the "Event" at Southwark Park came to an end each year I would play very patriotic songs, "Jerusalem" "Land of hope and glory" "Rule Britannia" to accompany the firework display that would start as soon as the main act had finished, this was always a great way to finish, as thousands of local people filed out of the park, probably to their local pub to continue the partying. This year 2022, Southwark council cancelled our carnival, due to lack of funds, are we going to let this happen again? One day a year the community, comes together to celebrate Bermondsey and all the different cultures that live here. We need our carnival returned to the organisers Bermondsey beat, they have always done a fantastic job, give them a large budget and let's see who will be appearing in the park next summer, come on Bermondsey let's get this party started.

I would like to take this opportunity to thank Bermondsey Beat for helping me fulfil my dream and become Bermondsey's number one DJ. Thanks Russell Dryden and Phil Burkett for the great memories, and please keep on organising the carnival for many more years to come.

If you think about it Bermondsey has produced some big stars, when I was growing up I looked up to people like Max Bygraves, Tommy Steele, Charlie Drake, Michael Caine just because they "come from round here", Bygraves insisted he was from Rotherhithe and Michael Caine was brought up in the Elephant and Castle, but would like a drink in the Bermondsey pubs, "There's not a lot of people know that!" Sorry couldn't resist that one, I think you know what I mean though.

Tommy Steele has always been a hero of mine "Singing the blues" "Little white bull" and my favourite "Half a sixpence", what a performer, and a great work ethic. I remember seeing him after watching the 1996 FA cup final at Wembley, Manchester United v Liverpool, Tommy is a big Liverpool fan and was getting chauffeured in a limousine away from Wembley after a 1-0 loss against United (Cantona). I was in a minibus full of cockney reds, we were heading for the "Gazebo" pub in Kingston to celebrate the victory. We were gesticulating to Tommy the score, amongst other things, and he looked up and gave us one of those famous smiles, he took it well. I would love to invite Tommy Steele to the Bermondsey carnival, just to say a few words on the mic, it would be great, wouldn't it?

Scott Lidgett school produced Trevor Aylott, who played up front for Chelsea, he managed Bromley fc and I remember he had a fight with Bryan Kidd in a Man City v Chelsea game and got sent off. Johnny Bumstead was a pupil of St Michaels (my school) and went on to captain Chelsea and Charlton.

Bermondsey boy, and a good friend of mine Michael Marks holds the record for the youngest player to score a hattrick for Millwall. He was playing alongside Teddy Sheringham at the time. A serious injury cut short his career. In the showbiz world, Michael Barrymore, who I worked with at the Bermondsey carnival, it was quite funny, I was preparing to announce him onto the stage for his special appearance and he was standing behind me, but out of site. I began by saying "Ladies and gentlemen, we now have a very special guest here this afternoon, one of the most famous icons ever to be produced in Bermondsey, it gives me great pleasure to welcome on stage…Zampa the Lion!" well, Michael's face was a picture, and he laughed as Zampa (The Millwall mascot) trundled past him, to the sound of "Let em come"

Like Michael Barrymore, Jade Goody was brought up on the Dickens Estate, Peter Butler house, right next to the ship aground in Dockhead. Let's not forget, Jade finished 4th in the Big Brother house, but she ended up the richest out of the lot of them. And I can tell you why, she was herself, she didn't comply, she was always herself, take it or leave it, most people took it and enjoyed her refreshing honesty. I loved her, and cried for her kids when she died, I went to her funeral down the blue and so did many thousands of us, this, my friends is what Bermondsey is all about. We are very proud of our successes and Jade Goody was very much a success. Life is so cruel sometimes, and Jade was taken far too soon, R.I.P Jade.

So many things have changed in Bermondsey, not least the pubs, My Favourite pub was always the "Lill" and it was one of the first music pubs to be turned into Flats, situated in Old Jamaica road with the junction of Abbey street, it still looks like the old "Lill" from the outside but inside the old pub is split into half a dozen apartments. So many old pubs have gone the same way, The George near St Michaels is a block of flats, it was owned by Eddie Read, who had great success with his greyhounds. The Swan and sugarloaf is an apartment block, so is the Dockhead stores. Nothing lasts forever, I used to work in the busiest Fish n chip shop in Bermondsey the "Venus Fish bar" I was just 17 and would sit down for my break after the busy teatime hour and help myself to cod n chips and a pickled gherkin. It was owned by a Greek family headed by Chris Alex and Bill, all very nice people, although Bill was an absolute "Bread n Butter" Chris was the Casanova of the three, he could pull a bird! After closing the Venus one night he took me to "Samantha's" nightclub, just off Regent Street, wow what a place, downstairs in the club the DJ booth was inside a red Jaguar E-type car, and the DJ would play while sitting in the driving seat. What a sound system! Bose speakers dotted all-round the place. Upstairs more speakers and beams of light illuminating the dance floor, it had more of a "Saturday night fever" look to it, and they played great dance tracks. Here I am, at the age of 17, and in a top west end nightclub, and my first drink was Scotch and coke, and to this day I have never changed, except I now call it a gold watch.

While I was working for them, I heard the news that Elvis Presley died suddenly of a heart attack, and John Lennon got shot dead in New York city. How's your luck? Two of the biggest pop stars in the history of music, and I was in the "Venus" when it happened. I later worked for Alex, who by the way, was a very nice man and like all the brothers, smoked far too much, down the farmhouse kitchen at the junction of Drummond Road and Jamaica road, it had an unusual but very popular menu, Faggots and peas pudding, Chicken Curry and rice, Scampi and chips, Spareribs it was all good stuff, and always kept very clean, like the Venus fish bar. The ques on a Friday night were legendary at both places.

I left the farmhouse kitchen and joined Christian &Co based in Shad Thames in the old decrepit wharfs that were used when the docks were thriving. The same ones that used to throw fresh fruit out of the loopholes when we were kids. I was a warehouse man and helped distribute advertising materials around the country. It was crazy because I just walked into the reception and asked if there were any jobs, and seconds later I was walking along Jamaica road with a new job.

After a few years at Christians the guvnor from the company next door asked if I would like to work for them, a company called Mobile merchandising, they were based in Shad Thames and they printed t-shirts for the music industry and they would sell them in places like Woolworths in a twelve inch format, so just like the album cover, but when you opened it up it was a t-shirt, the most famous and biggest seller, at the time was "Frankie say's Relax" in black letters, very simple design, but sold thousands. It was 1985 and this company also sold the "Live Aid" t-shirt for the concert, and I was one of the very few, that wore the shirt on the way to Wembley. I got "Live Aid" tickets from the boss at work and my friend John Sullivan came with me, what a gig that was! U2, David Bowie, Queen, The Who, that day, was one of the best of my life, this was a piece of history, one of the greatest ever concerts, and we was there! myself and John put away quite a few lagers during the day, we got back to Bermondsey, still thirsty, and both of us, high as a kite, we ended up at our mate Albert Lawson's pub, the Swan and sugarloaf, till the wee small hours.

Bermondsey has produced a few superstars and I am very proud of all of them. Danny Baker always used to drink in Bermondsey, one day I saw him down Mill Street in the Lanterna, with Chris Evans and Gazza a little worse for wear the lot of them. Danny was discovered by Janet Street Porter, and he has done very well for himself, if you get a chance check out his books, they are very entertaining. His radio shows were brilliant, and he has released several videos, but remember, I gave him his big break! Danny also helped behind the scenes with the Bermondsey carnival each year and would always give it airtime on his radio shows, by interviewing Bermondsey beat's Phil Burkett. Peter Kay played Danny's dad in the sitcom "Cradle to the grave" I loved this show, and I must admit I fell in love with his French teacher Miss Blondell, played by Julie Dray, she played that part very well I thought.

Eddie Webber was my best mate at St Joseph's RC school in George row, Bermondsey. We held the record of going up for afters, apple crumble and custard, seventeen times! Those were the days. Eddie has had a fabulous acting career in the theatre, and in classic films like "The Firm" and "The Business" he has also appeared in tv episodes of "The Bill", Birds of a feather" and "London's Burning". He recently had a part playing Phil Mitchell's mate in Eastenders, I hope the role expands, and he becomes a regular in the show with his good friend Danny Dyer. I recall he made a very popular advert for the tv on the first sign of having a stroke, it showed Eddie with a flame on his temple, that was getting larger, with his face starting to hang. The commentary suggesting, we all look out for the first signs, and possibly save a person's life.

David Haye was brought up down Long Lane, Bermondsey and was a terrific boxer, I followed his fights, and was a big fan, but he was a cruiser weight really, and the heavyweight division was too tough for him, especially when he got injuries that effected his mobility in the ring, in other words he stopped dancing, bobbing and weaving, and became a standing target, in the past he could skip around and avoid the jabs, unfortunately the injuries hampered his career and he had to call it a day, it's a shame, but that is the way the cookie crumbles.

Max Bygraves was another Bermondsey/Rotherhithe boy that done very well indeed, he learned it the hard way with Eric Sykes and Frankie Howard helping him to write comedy sketches. He was a comedian and a great mimic, but his singing was his best trait. He became a pop star, with lots of hits in the chart, he turned to a singalongamax style, by singing medleys of wartime songs, and traditional songs, and it worked big time. He was the host of "Sunday night at the London Palladium", which was the most popular variety show on tv at the time. He also took over from Bob Monkhouse as host to "Family fortunes" Max died in Australia in August 2012.

The biggest change to Bermondsey in recent times must be the Jubilee line extension and the opening of Bermondsey Tube station, the year was 2000, and yes 22 years ago it opened! Incredible how time flies by. I use it every day, and it is amazing to think how we got by before. All we had was the 47 and 188 bus, or you could jump into an executive car courtesy of Dockhead cars, if you were very lucky, you would have Charlie overcoat take you to the theatre in his nicotine infested motor! Bermondsey bods these days love nothing better than to jump on the Jubilee to Bond Street and buy a pair of Gucci suede moccasins or slip into Burberry and get a scarf. But seriously, I know you're not going to believe it, but I have a freedom pass, yes, I know you can't believe I am sixty, but if you pardon the pun, "the world is my oyster card" and now, ladies and gentlemen the Elizabeth line is open and it's going to make it easier to get to Heathrow, with shorter traveling times. The Bermondsey tube station has definitely improved this area, big time.

Now I am throwing a swerve ball here, but his dad was born and bred on Jamaica road, and to me that is good enough to make Zak Crawley a honouree Bermondsey boy. So ok, He went to Tonbridge School, and that is a bit posh for us Bermondsey folk, but his dad is proper Bermondsey and made it good in the futures market over the city, so anyway, it's my book, and what I say goes. If you don't know, Zac plays domestically for Kent and test cricket for England as an opening batsman, and I believe he will become the greatest English batsman of all time, no pressure then. He once scored 267 against Pakistan in 2021 and during the game it was fun texting his uncle Richard, who I know very well, we were both nervous for him as he edged to his double century. I put a poster up on the "Bermondsey radio" Facebook group page to mark his great achievement. I would like to wish Zac all the best for a long record-breaking career for Kent and England.

Barry Albin Dyer is, and always will be Mr Bermondsey, a man of true class and standing in our community. He put my Mum and Dad to rest with style and respect and now his sons Simon and Jon are carrying on to the very high standards that their Father set. One of my greatest honours was to play music at Barry's surprise 60th birthday party in a posh hotel in London's west end, wow, they picked me! This was like playing to Bermondsey royalty, I remember Father Alan, from Dockhead Holy Trinity church sang a song on this special evening, it was Elton John's "Can you feel the love tonight" from the film soundtrack The Lion King, it brought a standing ovation at the end of his rendition. At the end of this amazing night I was packing my DJ equipment away and I got a polite tap on the shoulder, It was Barry behind me, I looked round, he took my hand, shaking it, and said to me "Noel, that was one of the best nights ever, thank you for playing such wonderful music" Well, I was delighted to have made his special surprise 60th a success, It's the least I could do, Look what he had been doing for us, the people of Bermondsey all his life. If you get the chance get his book "Don't drop the coffin" it's a great read.

I am proud, I framed a speech that was spoken by our MP at the time Simon Hughes, in the chamber of the house of commons, I went to Albins head office in Culling Road, SE16 and presented it to them, it was regarding the award to Barry Albin Dyer, of an OBE in 2010. They were over the moon with my kind gesture of framing the speech. It was my small way of saying thank you for what he and his staff did for my Mum and Dad when they laid them to rest, all those years ago.

Barry Albin Dyer passed away on 6th June 2005 and we miss him very much indeed.

I love Australia, if I won a fortune on the lottery, it would be, see you later Alligator. I'm off. My second trip to Australia was completely different to my first trip. My sister had bought a place there, so when I arrived in Melbourne, I had a place to stay, which was well wicked. My sister Lorraine and her husband George now had a place right next to the Crowne Casino, which is right in the centre of town, I decided to visit Australia for the tennis at the Rod Laver arena, so off I went. My first night there I went to see a match in the BIG Bash cricket, with my brother-in-law George Snr, and his son, my nephew George, always well attended these games, but the jetlag was getting to me, and rather than go out on the lash after the game, I had to call it a day and gets some kip. Next morning, I went for a tour at Melbourne cricket ground, I had been there before, when I was in Australia the first time, I went to see Shane Warne and Ricky Pontin play for their state sides, Melbourne V Tasmania, this was just before the ashes series started and the 100,000 spectators that would pack themselves into this ground on Boxing Day test were nowhere to be seen. Only a couple of hundred were inside to watch a bore draw. The tour of the MCG was very good, went all over the ground, up in the gods, in the media box, the dressing rooms and even on the pitch. On the way out I grabbed an authentic Kookaburra ball in the souvenir shop and gave it as a gift to my brother-in-law George, He loved it.

The Crowne Casino is within spitting distance of George and Lorraine's place, they all know I am not a gambler, so the blackjack and roulette tables did not interest me in the casino across the road, but this place had cinemas, a theatre, a night club, loads of bars and restaurants, it was massive, not as big as the ones in Vegas, but big enough. I would often go over to the casino to the famous food halls, they would have cuisines from all over the world, and at reduced prices to keep you in there gambling, I'd pop over for a take-away and the portions were plentiful but cheap. Chinese was my favourite, with spareribs to die for. St Kilda is just a short tram ride away from the busy centre of Melbourne and is like going back in time to Margate of the seventies, a massive sandy beach with crashing waves, ideal for surfers, and a fun fare with Ferris wheel, dodgems, and roller-coaster. They had candy-floss stalls, Hot dogs and Kfc not forgetting the Fish and Chips. The smells were amazing, I spent the whole day there on the beach in the sunshine.

Watching Sport was really a good way of spending the day outside for very little money, I had day and night tickets for several dates for the Australian open tennis at the Rod Laver arena and it was such a great time out. My tickets were all in great positions around the centre court and I remember I got a text from back home saying they had just seen me on Sky News during a tennis report. 12,000 miles from home and I'm on the telly! It was a great experience I watched Nadal, Federer, Djokovic, (when he was allowed in the country) the beautiful Sharapova, and Simona Halep, my previous visit to the Rod Laver arena I watched Carole King in concert. I already had tickets for a one-day cricket match between Australia and England in Sydney, the cricket was cancelled but I had accommodation and flights booked so I went anyway, I walked around Sydney and came across a theatre showing a production of "Wicked", the prequel to the Wizard of Oz, it was brilliant, very funny, and the costumes and effects were spot on. Yes, if I win the lottery, someday soon, there is a place I will be going to, and that is somewhere in Australia.

New York was next on my list, it was St Patricks weekend, and it did not disappoint, I flew with United airlines into JFK and got a cab into the city, my hotel was very near Carnegie Hall, 7th Avenue on 55th street called The Wellington hotel, it was where Borat made that naked wrestling scene with his agent in the movie of the same name. It was a good hotel, and I would recommend it, my room had a double bed a microwave a tv and a nice shower room, it was St Patricks weekend, and it was freezing cold, I would say it was brass monkey weather, but that wouldn't give it justice, I have never been colder in my life when I went and stood on Broadway watching the St Patricks day march, I was well wrapped up believe you me, but after about two hours watching I had to bail out, and find a bar open, It took me just a few minutes to find an Irish bar, right next to my hotel and ordered my first of many pints of Guinness, it was the first bar with an internet juke box, meaning, I could play any track I fancied, I always tipped the barman and this meant that when I asked for another drink he was on my case straight away, I got slightly drunk that day, on the way back to the hotel I stopped at a very famous pizzeria franchise, and its name escapes me but they were everywhere in New York, I thought to myself I better eat something before I hit the sack or I'm going to be tom and dick (sick) in the morning, and I had lots more to see in this magnificent place. I made a fatal schoolboy error when I ordered my Pepperoni pizza, I said to the waitress "Can I have a LARGE pepperoni, deep pan please" The waitress looked at me as though I was mad and replied, "Did you say large pepperoni deep pan sir?" Others waiting for their orders to be finished turned around at me shaking their heads in disbelief. Thirty minutes later I was clinging onto a square box that was massive, hot, and difficult to manoeuvre, and I had to put it on its side to get out the door. It was freezing on the way back to the Wellington, as I passed the receptionist behind the desk she quipped "You hungry sir?" I laughed, and I have no idea how I got it in the lift, I placed it on the bed when I got into my room and opened the lid, wow, I could only eat almost half of it, and had the rest the next afternoon for lunch. The moral of this story is never order large pizza in America unless you're sharing.

The next morning was less cold, and I was on a mission to have a look round this famous city, first I got into a taxi and headed for the Staten Island ferry, this was the best way of passing the statue of liberty and getting a selfie as it passes over your shoulder behind you. The thing is, when you get to the island, you get off and straight back on, to return to the quayside that you boarded the ferry in the first place. I walked up into the business district and noticed a large bronze charging bull, just around the corner was "ground zero", where the twin towers once stood proudly, now there was just an empty space, I ventured into a department store that was famous for designer goods at very low prices, I couldn't resist a couple of Ralph Lauren shirts, I started walking back up through little Italy and I was feeling the strain on my plates of meat (Feet), I hailed a cab and asked him to take me to "Grand central station" wow it was impressive, beautiful architecture, I had a coffee first and took it all in, then made my way to the "Oyster bar", this place is world famous and I ordered a dozen under advice from the Bar tender, he put me right, and they were devoured very eagerly, and they were lovely. It was around midday, and I decided to get the Rockefeller centre and the Empire state building in before I called it a day. So, arriving at the Rockefeller it was a very modern looking building and inside the lifts took you up to the viewing gallery very quickly, it was like a rocket! I bought a fantastic t-shirt with workers sitting on an iron girder high above the ground, I loved that shirt, if I go back, I'll buy another one. The view was fantastic of New York, the viewing gallery was 360 degrees, and I could see for miles including Central Park in the distance. The Empire state building was a different kettle of fish, I think I remember the first lift took you up so far, and the second lift took you to the top, and a much smaller gallery with viewing binoculars on stands and available by putting a coin into the slot. While I was up there, just a few minutes, I couldn't help thinking of King Kong clinging on to this part of the building as the USA fired machine guns from the twin winged aircrafts and eventually Kong lost his grip and fell to the ground below. Yes, I know it was a movie, but I was in the moment, I also thought of those people that were even higher up in the twin towers, that were felled by those terrorists in two planes crashing into them. That was part of the reason I visited New York to see for myself ground zero. It was silent spacious and being rebuilt when I visited, hopefully I can return get my Rockefeller t-shirt, and witness the new skyscrapers that have taken their place one day. That night I went to see a show on Broadway, it was a show featuring the music and life story of Johnny Cash, who had recently died, there wasn't much dialogue, but the music was great, although the show closed after just 2 weeks, they call these show's "juke box" and consist of music throughout, and very little dialogue. New York city and country music don't really go together, so this show was never going to last. I went to see Spamalot, a musical comedy about the Holy grail and Monty Pythons comedy version of it, this show was very funny indeed and I was sitting next to American's that adore anything Monty Python. In my entire life I have never seen people laughing so hysterically. The middle-aged lady next to me was holding her tummy and tears of laughter were rolling down her face, I was laughing at the audience reaction because it was so infectious, yes that was one hell of an experience, top notch.

And finally, the best of the lot, now I don't like opera, but boy did I love Phantom of the Opera on Broadway, are you kidding me? From the moment the lights in the theatre dimmed I was almost forcing myself to frown upon it and not enjoy it. If you don't do nothing else go and see this show it is just brilliant. The music, the vocal performances, special effects, it is just incredible. It moves you, and the hairs on the back of my neck stood to attention 10 out of 10. I tried to get tickets for the Pogue's on St Patricks day night to no avail, can you imagine what that would have been like? but my trip to the big apple was fantastic, I would like to go back and get my Rockefeller t-shirt and see the new towers in place. I found the American people to be nice to talk to, they love the British and I love them.

Lee Thompson is the saxophonist with the ska band and British institution MADNESS and when he is not playing with them, he has a band behind him called the Camden cowboys, one year they performed at the Bermondsey carnival and boy can he play the Sax! I went up to him backstage and asked him if I could play some ska classics before they took to the stage. "Yes, he said, play some specials if you like" he said enthusiastically. "Leave it to me" I said confidently. The sun was shining, and I slipped on some music from the beat, The Specials, The Selector, and even a bit of Bad manners, it all went down a treat. When the Camden cowboys came on stage, they took the crowd with them on a musical journey that was full of beats and ska classics, they performed a few Madness tunes, Night boat to Cairo, one step beyond, it was a great set and Lee Thompson came across as a nutty boy, but a very nice man.

Stacey Solomon appeared at the carnival when we moved to the Bandstand, she was an X Factor finalist and sung in the semi-final with Michael Bublé and the song they sung was an old Nina Simone classic "Feeling good", so I went to her Winnebago tapped on the open door and there she was sitting before me, "Before you go on, can I play feeling good, the song you did with Michael Bublé on X Factor?" I asked, "Yes" she said "That's a good idea" so I did, and the crowd loved it too, Stacey did very well if you consider it was all on backing tapes, but she was a lovely lady and came across very well. I don't even watch X Factor, but I did my homework and discovered she sang it in the semi-final of the show with Bublé. These small things make all the difference when dealing with professional performers.

I worked with "The Real thing" twice, once in the park, and the second time on the bandstand, these guys are great fun to be around, always Larkin about. They have had some big hits in the seventies and eighties, and they perform them very well "You to me are everything" is my favourite, I have played it so many times, I wish I had a penny for every time I had played it, I'd be loaded. Dressed in matching blue tracksuits, they belted out "Can you feel the force" "Can't get by without you" and they really worked the crowd well.

Rose Royce had a lot of success in the UK with hits like "Car wash" "Wishing on a star" the lady that sung those songs was Gwen Dickey, she was a little nervous, and Phil Burkett from Bermondsey beat had to escort her on stage, once she started, she was amazing, the Bermondsey crowd loved her, and duly got a great ovation at the end of their set.

Bermondsey carnival one year had one of my favourite disco bands when I was growing up, Heatwave had a fantastic back catalogue of hits, and my song was "Always and forever" loved it. Rod Temperton was the original keyboard player and wrote most of their songs until Quincy Jones got hold of him. He wrote songs on Michael Jacksons albums as well as stuff for George Benson and the Brothers Johnson, but even though there were no original band members left in the band on that day, they sounded good, and the vocalist was excellent. "Boogie nights" and "Mind blowing decisions" went down very well.

Alexander O'Neal had to cancel his first appearance at the carnival because a young lad got stabbed at the front of the stage, Alexander was standing behind me, just about to go on. I had worked the crowd up with some dance classics, and the police arrived and said he couldn't go on. A couple of years later he came back and did manage to get on stage, I believe he didn't do his full hour that he was booked for, He sang "Criticize" and "Saturday love" and after just 40 minutes came off, and when I said to him "Are you going back on?" He replied, "I have another booking at Newbury racecourse, I got to go" Now you know why he is no longer one of my favourites. I must say that working with these stars has taught me to appreciate each gig, I love what I do, it gives me a big buzz when I connect with the crowd, hopefully I can continue for many years to come. You're not getting rid of me just yet.

My Top five concerts of all time are as follows, number FIVE was Prince at the O2 arena in North Greenwich, he was appearing at this venue for several nights, and I must admit, I was a bit worse for wear (too many gold watches) but even so, he was excellent. A fifteen-minute version of purple rain was the highlight, but he could sing, he could dance, but he was one hell of a guitar player.

Number FOUR was the Rolling Stones at Twickenham stadium, it was a wonderful summers night, and I had a great seat overlooking the stage, and the boys did not disappoint, an acoustic version of Angie was one of my favourites, but Sympathy for the devil always wins it for me, lots of audience participation throughout, Mick Jagger strutting all over the giant stage set. I am so glad that I got to see them before it was too late.

Number THREE was The Boss Bruce Springsteen at Wembley stadium and the Born in the USA tour. What a performer. This was my first time seeing the Boss, I have seen him many more times since, he is one of the best you will ever see, the musicians are fantastic, and the sound is magnificent. Add Bruce with three and a half hours of great tunes and you have one hell of a show.

Number TWO was the Live Aid concert at Wembley stadium a week after I saw Bruce Springsteen in the Born in the USA tour. The start with Status Quo was iconic and the sheer number of stars that appeared was mouth-watering. The Who, Bowie, U2 it was relentless, but I have to say Queen stole it for me, when they sang radio ga ga it was visually stunning, as everyone clapped their hands in sync above their heads. To be there was a privilege and an honour.

Number ONE at Wembley stadium the greatest performer of all time Michael Jackson Dangerous Tour, saw it three times, out of this world. This guy was on another level, perfectionist a great showman and the sound was incredible. When Billy and Angie were leaving the Lill, I gave Angie and her daughter Sally two tickets for one of the dates of the Dangerous tour, it was a small thank you for all the work they had given me over the years. Angie shed a tear when she opened the envelope and young Sally was ecstatic, I was pleased I made them so happy on a very sad day, leaving the Lill must have been hard. Just a few years ago Angie passed away, we all miss her very much indeed.

I have been very lucky and not been to many bad concerts, very rarely have I walked out of a gig I have paid good money to see. I am a music fan, and I will stay and see it through to the end on most occasions. But the worst concert I have ever seen was at Hyde Park a few years back, the star was Madonna, and she was awful, two hours into the set I recognised just one song "Hung up" the rest of it was album tracks I had never heard of, and never want to hear again. There was a lot of simulated sex going on in her act on stage, and at one point she was interfering with herself. I was looking forward to hearing "Into the groove" but this was taking it to another level.

Steely Dan wasn't much better at the Wembley arena in the early eighties, but at least they didn't use a crucifix!

It baffles me how big stars with a large catalogue of hits, turn up on a world tour and churn out album tracks, or even worse "I am now going to play tracks from my new album" People are paying good money to see their greatest hits and when they turn up, they get obscure album tracks. It's a nightmare, Friends have told me they have seen this behaviour from David Bowie, Elton John, Madonna, Rod Stewart, they are all at it. It's a bit like going to a party knowing that Bermondsey's number one DJ is playing the tunes, and all you hear is Olly Murs songs, you would be furious, wouldn't you? Can I assure you all, that is never going to happen. I would never play any Olly Murs songs; I have a reputation to live up to. So, all you megarich superstars, do yourself a favour, and play the greatest hits, and look after your fans. Because that's what I intend to do, play the songs they want to hear.

Noel – Bermondsey's number one DJ

The Throb Mob Left to right bottom row Carly Britton Wendy Fitzgerald Kerrie Pooke Yvette Chandler Top left to right Keely Brown Emma Bowers Lynne Damiral Katy Hansen Colette Savage. Bottom picture of Stansfeld football club our sponsor next page Me and Zampa at the Bermondsey Carnival, and The Champagne dancers on the MV La Palma. Alison, Abi, Nicki, Louise, and Karen.

CHAPTER NINE

GOA - A PASSAGE TO INDIA

India is like Marmite, you either like it or you hate it, on the dark side, it is corrupt, especially the old bill, it is polluted beyond your wildest imagination, and the most obvious one, it is very dirty, they defecate in the streets. On the light side, it is cheap beyond belief if you are a bit squeaky or don't like spending money, this place is for you. The beauty of some of the beaches is outstanding and the beaches in Goa go on for miles. You can get your Hampstead's done for a couple of grande and return home looking like Donny Osmond. You can eat like a king and pay peanuts. The people of India are its jewel, they are kind, and love the English, I am a person who sees his glass half full, so therefore I visit India every year, it is a magical place, a spiritual place, in this chapter I shall explain why I keep going and why you should try it out, like me, you could fall in love with the place.

Micky Saunders, otherwise known as Tat, for many years kept on at me, telling me "Noel, you'd love it in Goa" he would describe how I could DJ there in front of thousands! That sounded appealing, but never really materialised, but it sounded good at the time. He kept on at me and eventually I cracked and decided to book a trip to Goa, I booked a return flight with Thomas cook and started planning. I needed a Malaria inoculation from my GP and that was sorted for the price of a prescription, the next bit was a bit more complicated, the visa, there are many different types, but I went for one that you apply for online and it's called a tourist visa, my current visa runs out in a couple of years, I couldn't use it during the pandemic, so I may be able to use it this February if everything goes to plan. The first question from you all is why don't a lot of holiday makers travel to Goa? The simple reply to that is they must fill in complicated paperwork for the visa, and get a jab for Malaria, this puts off a lot of people before they have booked a flight, which is nine hours long, this could put them off too. Some people don't like to fly for nine hours. It's an expensive flight, but everything else is unbelievably cheap. If you like holidaying in Marbella, wearing designer clothes, and Gucci shoes, then India is not for you. Dress code is very relaxed, t-shirt, shorts, and flip flops will get you in most places and so think about these points before you decide to book a flight, then you can commit to an adventure of a lifetime.

Goa has a holiday season beginning in October and running through to the end of April, then it quickly turns to the rainy season. The average temperature throughout their holiday period is 90 degrees Fahrenheit, October till April, you might get the odd shower, but they would be very rare. I travel to a resort called Candolim and have an apartment that I use all the time, it is two hundred yards from the beach and is equipped with giant tv, air conditioning, fridge, double bed, and shower for just £12 per night and you can get a lot cheaper too. The dress code in Goa is that there is none, I have seen people wear the same t-shirt two days on the spin, a definite no no in Marbella. No designer clothes, no Gucci, no Prada, no Ralph its very casual, a fruit of the loom £2.99 t-shirt, pair of shorts and some sand shoes, wallop you're ready to go out. Taxis are cheap, but a tuk tuk is even cheaper, I have trouble getting my fat frame into one, but when I do, I must save myself pennies. Agree a price before you get in the motor. Eating out is fantastic, very cheap, and sea food is very good value, but they serve Buffalo steaks in some restaurants as they are not allowed to serve beef steak, the Hindu religion means Cows are worshipped, and therefore not mistreated in any way, they roam the streets, beaches, fields and must not be disrespected, or you could face jail. There are a lot of medical tourists in Goa, especially for teeth, I will explain later my experience, I had 16 teeth porcelain veneers and crowns, eight on top, eight on bottom, £100 a tooth and they are still looking good after five years. I had spectacles in Mont Blanc frames made to my prescription for peanuts.

Let's elaborate on these adventures in Goa, if you can look past the poverty and the misfortune of the locals, they survive on very little, you will see the absolute beauty of the place. The Indian people are very nice and there smiles light up the day with their kindness and generosity. Don't get me wrong, they will have you over if you are not paying attention, so watch out for the greedy ones, taxi drivers are the main culprits, get a good one, get his number and you be set up for a good time. My first visit to Goa was an eye opener, I arrived at the airport and a taxi driver, arranged by Micky, was waiting for me in the early hours of the morning. After an hour's drive we arrived at my apartment, on the outskirts of Candolim. I was on the first floor and the door had a padlock, and all the windows had bars to prevent intruders. This was the same with all properties. My place was spacious with a double bed, fridge, shower, tv and air conditioning, the chairs in the lounge were very uncomfortable, like sitting on wooden crates, with pillows made of straw. Outside it was pitch black, couldn't see much just silhouettes of buildings and trees. I unpacked and got into bed, the driver had told me, Micky would be coming round at 10am to see me, so I better get some shut eye.

Micky is the nicest warmest, most generous person I have ever met, and he knows Goa like the back of his hand, he tends to exaggerate a lot, he will tell you over the phone that he is in a bar in Calangute and "It is absolutely buzzing!" and when you get there, he is there with just three other people! And he does this a lot. Micky is also the number one deejay in Goa and always insists that I am number two, which is fair enough, I have never heard anyone mix like Micky, especially on his tablet! Its mesmerising and can often put you into a trance, some people, actually fall asleep! I'm only joking Mick. Nah I'm not.

Micky turns up at 11am and after a quick chat and some financial formalities, he takes me to the Supermarket to stock up for the next few days, Water, chocolate, crisps, nuts, juices all go into the metal shopping basket, and Mickey puts a large packet of toilet rolls in as well, "I am only here for two weeks Mick!" I said, he retorted "Yeah, but you might get the shits!" and laughed out loud. "Cheers Mick" I said, I could feel a rumbling in my tummy already, and I hadn't eaten anything yet.

The rest of the day was spent at the "Boat Shack", eating, drinking, and meeting the gang. The Boat Shack is where I spend most my time, sunbathing and relaxing. Smiler is the manager and, you guessed it, doesn't stop smiling! He would do anything for you, and he is one of the gang. The first thing you notice in Goa is how cheap drinking and eating is, on my first day I drank loads of the local beer, kingfisher, had a curry and when I left five hours later my bill came to £7, I love it here already.

In the evening I got ready and went out for a meal, we were the only ones there but took up twenty covers, I ordered beef wellington (it was beef) and thoroughly enjoyed it, Chocolate mousse for afters, and the whole meal and drinks, it wasn't even a tenner, I think I have covered the prices here, you get the idea. We headed back to Candolim beach road and spent the rest of the night in one of the many bars along that road, a nice evening, and a great way of meeting everyone.

Next morning, I headed to the beach, I had arranged with Santos to sort me out a sun lounger away from anyone, my psoriasis is all over my body, so I am very shy and paranoid about people staring at me, factor thirty on, and I remain under the umbrella for a few days, the redness fades away and I start to look more normal. I start most sunshine holidays like this, but the first few days I feel like a leper. But if my fellow holiday makers don't like my skin, I am trying my best. The food in the boat shack is out of this world, but they can't do sausages or bacon, and experienced travellers import their breakfasts in suitcases on their flight out. My start to the day is normally a visit to the coconut stall and the young lads would use a machete to cut open the shell for a straw to slip in, and the great taste of the coconut water. A short walk to the boat shack, and my usual order would be plain omelette, beans on toast, fresh orange juice a mug of coffee and honey for my omelette. always did the trick and never caused any strange bowel movements. For lunch my favourite is butter chicken, which is a bit like chicken masala, but much creamier. Accompanied by a garlic nan and pilau rice. Banana fritters and ice-cream for afters, then back to the sunbed to get some rays till sunset.

Taxis at the airport are hit or miss, it costs around £12 to Candolim but the driving to your destination can be, let's say hazardous, on one occasion we agreed a price and I suggested that if I get to Candolim before sunset I would give him a three quid tip, well I promise you, the driver was like a man possessed,, the best way of describing his driving, he was auditioning for stunt driver for the next Bond film, you know those opening sequences that end with the chasing vehicle going over the side of a cliff, rolling down to bottom of a gauge, and bursting into flames. I was clinging on in the back seat, being tossed around like a rag doll, he was going up banks on the side of the highway, overtaking with inches to spare with oncoming traffic. We arrived after sunset, it took longer than it normally would, and my heart was pumping and wanted to get out of the vehicle. Sod it, I gave him his tip, left my case in my room, and headed for the first bar I could find, ordered a large scotch and coke, it didn't touch the sides, welcome to Goa. On another occasion at the airport, a different driver, and I offered the same incentive, this guy said he knew a "Shortcut". Well, he eventually got me to my apartment three hours later, I thought he was kidnapping me! I saw road signs for Mumbai for God's sake, that's on the way home!

Mahi Desai is the owner of Goa Dental studio in Calangute and what a fantastic dentist she is, since I was a kid, I always had discoloured teeth, my mum was taking a certain drug while pregnant with me, and it affected the colour of my smile, not very attractive. I decided to go see her and made an appointment when I arrived in Goa. We chatted about the procedure, and I agreed a price of £100 a tooth and set a date for next morning. I was having Porcelain Veneers and crowns fitted on top of my existing gnashers, this was going to be done in 2 visits. The next morning, I got a tuk tuk to the studio and was welcomed by Mahi, who showed me to her dentist chair, it was all very professional and soon I was laying back and a few strong injections were inserted into my gums and Mahi did her stuff. A couple of hours later I was sitting up in the chair with a temporary set of teeth in me gob, my mouth was numb and the whole procedure didn't hurt a jot, I made an appointment for a few days later, while the new smile was being made in the laboratory. When I went out that night, I discussed it all with Martin Dean, a top bloke, along with his wife Rebecca, they both had treatment previously and gave me top notch advice. I will never forget the way they welcomed me into the gang.

I made my way back to the studio for the final part of the process, the temps had to be removed, and the permanent ones glued in place, this took more injections and a few hours later .... BOSH! I left Mahi's looking like Donny Osmond! with a brilliant white smile, she did a wonderful job, and five years later they still look good.

Billy Bird is one hell of a dancer, and life and soul of any party. Whenever we met up somewhere, Bar, nightclub or in the boat shack, Billy would be first up on the dance floor. Billy has a great smile and personality, and his dance moves are out of this world. He would dance to anything with a beat, and naturally would make all the girls get up and boogie with him. Whenever Micky organised a party, he would invite everyone of course, but you had to invite Billy, he was the main man. Whenever I was in Goa there would be at least one party a day, sometimes two and Micky would go to them all, and be the last to leave. He is the ultimate party person, each season in Goa Micky would attend loads of raves, reggae, house, jungle, techno, acid house parties and get everyone involved. I would go, if they were playing "normal" music, I hate all that rave shit, Clockwork orange, I'd rather suck an orange, give me Lou Rawls any day.

The last time I was in Goa was January 2020, just a couple of months before lockdown, I stayed for three weeks, it was a great holiday. My 59th birthday party went down well, it took place at the boat shack on Candolim beach, I hired two fire eaters and organised a firework display, it didn't come to a rubber soap! (Cheap) I was pleased with the turn out, and the drinks flowed that night. Nice to see Anji and John, and my good friends Peter and Michael and not forgetting Billy Bird.

The boat shack looked after us, Sebby, who is the owner, and his wife let me plug my laptop into their sound system and we had a nice selection of tunes blasting out towards the sea. When it got dark the fire eaters took to the sand, down at the bottom of the steps to the shack and did a fifteen-minute set of blowing flames out of their mouths, and juggling balls that were on fire!

The fireworks were twenty minutes in duration, mainly whites and reds and hardly comparable to Sydney harbour bridge on New Year's Eve, but as I said it was cheap as chips.

Victor's is a sea food restaurant in Candolim, and it is my favourite place for sea food in the world, one time I had a "Sea food platter", my god! It could have fed four! Lobster, tiger prawns, crab, it was so tasty, oh my god it's making my mouth water just thinking about it. When you book at Victor's, you order your fish the day before, or the morning of the meal so he can order accordingly with the fishermen, no waste, and everything is caught that day. The décor is simple the place is basically just a large white tent, with maybe ten or twelve tables, very basic outdoor, but a top-notch place. There are so many Michelin star restaurants in Goa, all different types of cuisines and all at incredible prices, you will be spoilt for choice.

There is a massive supermarket at the top of "Beach Road" used by the tourists, the locals like to shop at their own markets, with even greater bargains to be had. Opposite the supermarket is the Elephant shop, this place you can buy a mobile and get connected to a network for silly money. Get your pound sterling changed into Indian rupee's, buy twenty Benson and Hedges for two quid, its like an Aladdin's cave of goodies and is used by so many tourists. Most visitors to Goa are British, with very few Europeans, but there are lots of Russians, although the locals don't like them because they are rude and don't tip.

India is five and a half hours in front of British time, this means if a Premiership match kicks off at 3pm, it will be shown live in most bars at 8.30pm in the evening, its big business, and I am pleased to say, there are no football shirts worn and everyone is well behaved. On Sunday's, so many places serve traditional British "Sunday lunch", some are very good indeed.

CHAPTER TEN

When Irish eyes are smiling

My Mum and Dad were both from Ireland, but my dad's side of the family is a mystery, I don't know if I have an aunt or uncle, cousins, gran, or grandad, and to be honest, I don't think I will ever find out. However, on my Mum's side I know quite a lot, including my mum's uncle John Oxx, a very famous Irish horse trainer, who trained Sinndar, Alamshar, and the greatest of them all Sea the stars. When I was very young, I remember my gran and grandad would hug me and my sister Lorraine when we arrived each summer, I can feel the love to this day, they loved us so much, and we loved them too. I have fond memories of them both. They owned a farm in Westminstown, near Lucan, County Dublin. Very close to where David and Victoria Beckham got married in Luttrellstown castle. It is kind of funny that when I followed Manchester united home and away, with the London supporters branch of Mufc, I would be on the same coach as Ted and Sandra Beckham, his mum and dad. They would get pestered for autographs by others on the coach but were very good about it. I was sitting next to them in old Trafford when David scored his first goal for Manchester united, it was in a Champions league game against Galatasaray, what a moment! I'll never forget it, shaking their hands and congratulating them.

Because my dad worked for British rail, he got free rail travel for all of us, and all the family went to Ireland for the summer holidays each year. Imagine a city kid from Bermondsey feeding my grandads pigs in the sheds, and out in the fields picking all the crops for market. I would play with my Irish cousins, mostly Trina, who was a little older than me, we would have a record player in our gran's farmhouse, and she would play K-tel compilation albums, with tracks from Slade, Sweet and Dave Edmunds, Who I would later share the stage with, at the Bermondsey carnival. I would trek over the fields to my uncle Noel and auntie Helen's house, and play with my cousins Martin and Margaret, what fun we would have picking raspberries and blackberries in the hedges along the narrow country lanes. My auntie Helen has appeared on an RTE game show, and won a car and a few euros, she is a lovely lady, with a heart of gold, and is there any chance of a loan auntie Helen? (I'm joking). My late uncle Noel was a gentleman, with a fantastic sense of humour, and I miss his brilliant smile.

In later years my cousins and I would be getting drunk in Kenny's bar in Lucan town centre along with Pauline and Tony, we all liked a drink, and would end up in Temple bar for late drinks. My cousins Pauline, Mags, and Tony brought me out for a drive one day and ended up in my late uncle Sean's pub "The Fox's Den", it was on the border of Limerick and Tipperary, and it would be where the fox hunters would meet on boxing day each year. It is a nice pub but miles away from anywhere, great views of the green fields surrounding the pub on both sides. But you needed to drive to it, and park up in the car park. Even the local off duty police officers would be found in the bar at two in the morning, then drive home. I must try and go back and see my Auntie Mary, who still runs the pub with her son Tony.

I have spent St Patricks day in New York city, and it was brilliant, very cold, but it was brilliant. But I have never been so drunk or seen so many people drunk in all my life when I went to Dublin's fare city for St Patricks day, it was a good few years back. Believe you me, I am trying to recollect what happened, but it is all a bit of a blur. The pubs must have opened at six in the morning because I do recall three lads stumbling through Temple bar at 11.30am as though they had been on the black stuff all night! Surely not, not in Ireland. It was a bank holiday and me Tony, Mags, Pauline, and a few of her friends started the drinking at around ten that day, we got the bus into town and there we saw the three lads bumping into lampposts and the walls and I thought to myself, this is going to be a heavy session, and it was. Musicians everywhere playing Irish tunes or as some people say, "fiddley dee music", I was drunk by two, my cousins must have thought I was a lightweight, and on that day, I was. I tried to sober up by eating something, it didn't help, and I was back in Lucan by six. I got a taxi back on my own. They stayed out all night. I felt so ill in the morning, my auntie Helen was laughing at the state I was in, but kindly made me an Irish breakfast, that aided my recovery big time. The rest of the stop outs were dying in their beds upstairs. There is one thing for sure to be sure, when I visit my relatives in Ireland and I return to Bermondsey, I need another week's holiday to recover my liver.

My uncle Eddie and auntie Mona were not only married to each other, but they were a double act, I mean a comedy double act, they were fantastic to me, unfortunately they have both passed away, I loved them dearly, so entertaining when I visited. I miss that banter.

One Sunday afternoon my uncle Eddie took me over to his club in Blanchardstown, he was a bit good at darts and beat me fairly and squarely and many times during the day. We were joined by his son Edward, my cousin, and he was with his girlfriend, we chatted about the good old days, and later that night, after the club called last orders, Edward asked me if I wanted to go out to the local nightclub, I fancied another drink, and I was encouraged by my uncle Eddie, so of we trot to this disco club, it was a Sunday night and it wasn't busy but somehow I started a conversation with a tall thin good looking Irish lady named Rose, she was more drunk than I was, and she was unbelievably on her own! Edward said he and his girlfriend were going home, and they asked if I was ok, I said I was, as I planted a cheeky kiss on Rose's cheek, I was aiming for her lips! Next thing I know I was in the reception of a hotel signing me and Rose in as Mr & Mrs Smyth. That is the first time and only time I kissed an Irish woman, and her name was Rose, it was very nice I remember, I'd love to do it again one day, if I am lucky enough. When I was a kid, we would go to church in

Lucan and after the service we would stop off at Hamrick's supermarket, a place where my auntie Josie worked, my grannie or grandad would give us 10p to get an ice-cream covered in chocolate, bit like a magnum, it was a nice treat after the church service. In later years when I visited Lucan, I would like to bring home some Galtee cheese in my suitcase it had a great taste. It reminded me of Ireland.

CHAPTER ELEVEN

THE BEGINNING OF THE END

This is the end of the first part of the book, the story of my colourful life leading us up to the 20^{th of} March 2020, it has everything in it, sentiment, fun, laughter, cruising, sex, music, Olympics, radio, India, New York, Australia, concerts, you name it, it's in it. I couldn't go straight into Bermondsey radio without telling you how it all fell into place. So not wishing to sound arrogant or big headed, how many deejays do you know that have their own radio station, to provide my community with much needed support throughout the pandemic. And now Written a book about my life and used the opportunity to thank the people that helped each other through this horrible time. I have played at top class London hotels, and all the pubs and tenants halls in SE16, appeared on stage with music stars that we all know and love. And who have I done this for? I did it for you, the people I care about, the people that cared enough to help me. You know who you are, too many to mention, when I was at rock bottom you helped me. I thank each and every one of you from the bottom of my heart.

There is so much more to write in this part of the book, but maybe in the future I may write a "Part 2" or a remix of this one, who knows. I hope you found it an interesting read, it came very naturally to me, and I am very surprised, as I didn't think I had any ability in writing an essay never mind a book!

Part 2 will begin next, and I will be dropping names of my listeners and characters on the radio, The Throb mob, my admin, the listeners, the sad times and the classic hilarious moments, part 2 is for you.

CHAPTER TWELVE

BERMONDSEY RADIO IS BORN

February 2020, I returned from Goa after three glorious weeks in the Indian sun, living and eating like a king, and not being able to spend my money. Came home with hundreds of pounds of holiday spending money. Had my teeth polished, bought some Mont Blanc designer frames, Lacoste shirts, my suitcase was full of good stuff, and I left the cheap stuff there. Not long after getting back into the swing of things at work, my van was broken into in the early hours of the morning, while I was at work. They took lighting mainly, which I have now replaced. But I have to say it is a terrible feeling finding my van's window smashed and rifled for its contents. My van has more locks on it now, so we carry on. But it was a big knock back, it demoralised me, but worse was yet to come, the covid 19 pandemic was about to hit home.

I was working for a company delivering stationary to the city of London Monday to Friday in the early hours of the morning, I would go in at 1am and be back home by 6am. I would deliver to lawyers and banks, and I enjoyed the hours, it gave me time in the day to get things done. I had recently returned from three weeks in Goa, India, I had an amazing time, and my skin looked a lot better. The sunshine does my Psoriasis a lot of good and I was already planning my next trip there, it would be my big sixtieth birthday! Little did I know that I was returning to England that already had recorded deaths from Covid19 and along with personal grief and hardship, this pandemic was going to be with us for a couple of years. I wasn't going to have a holiday for a very long time, and my skin was going to get a lot worse.

When I arrived home at Heathrow, after a nine-hour flight I noticed the airport was in higher alert mode, something different, I guessed it something to do with this covid 19 alert that was worrying all the world's governments. Things were looking bad in Italy, loads of deaths and it started to get serious in the UK towards the end of February. It was in the middle of March I thought to myself that this could get serious. We could be off work for a couple of weeks if Boris decides to lockdown the whole country. I had a couple of grand in savings and I could get through this if it doesn't last too long. The first thing I tought of was, Have I got enough toilet paper though?

We were all laid off work until further notice as a lockdown was announced for March 20th, 2020. This was now very real, deaths were going up and isolation was the key word, oh my god, what am I going to do? I had been experimenting with Facebook, trying to broadcast music mixes through my virtual DJ software on my laptop, and then "go live" on the Facebook network, after several attempts, they kept throwing me off due to the music copyrights issue. Lots of my friends would attempt to tune in to this but it kept on being interrupted by the Facebook authorities. Fair enough, so I tried to start a radio station, so I could play music to my friends and keep them amused during the next few weeks of boredom. This wasn't going to last too long, was it? Little did we know.

I searched Google with these few words "start my own radio station" and radio king came up, and this is where fate, good luck, Karma fell right into my lap. The software I downloaded from radio king was compatible with my Virtual DJ software that was on my laptop. Let me tell you straight, there was a lot of technical stuff to do to get "Bermondsey radio" on air and believe you me it was difficult. But to this day I don't know how I did it, but I did it.

I had an internet link that I shared on Facebook to my friends and by clicking on the link you could listen to my broadcast, on the same day as lockdown I broadcasted for a couple of hours and got five listeners! Sharon Saunders, Wendy Fitzgerald, Lee Ellis, and a married couple living in Tenerife Jean Barry and Dave London. I had played the tunes at their wedding reception down the Walworth Road just a couple of years previous. The crazy thing is, they were listening live out there in the Canary Islands, and they were in lockdown too. Bermondsey radio could be listened to in Perth Australia or Lewisham high street, all you needed to tune in was an internet connection by using your smart phone, tablet, laptop, even your internet connected tv.

In the first few days of broadcast all I did was play music, party songs mostly and then listeners would ask me to do a shout out to their mum, who they hadn't seen for a few days. I would record my voice and save it as a file using my phone, and when I was about to play their song, I would play the file. It sounded like I was talking on air "live", but I can assure you I wasn't. Wow they were so impressed, now, they all wanted a request. At this point the listener didn't know that this is how I was doing it, they thought I was using a microphone live, nope, not until another miracle took place. My flat is a mess, my mum, if she was alive would say it was a "pigsty", but that would be very unfair on all the pigs out there. My dining room table surface cannot be seen because of all sorts of shite upon it, one morning I was rummaging through the crap and found a usb lapel microphone, that is normally attached to your jacket lapel when making a recording for a blog or something. This couldn't possibly work with my laptop, could it? Oh, bloody hell yes! This tiny mic was the final piece in the jigsaw, and we now had a base to work from, and there was no limit to what we could achieve. To this day I am still using this very same lapel mic, it is hanging in there, just about. The laptop I use is a 17-inch Hewlitt Packard, an ancient model, and for the life of me I have no clue why, or how it is still working. I use it at my gigs, I use it daily to write this book, and for Bermondsey radio too. If you suddenly don't hear from me for a while, it will be the mic, or the laptop, or both go up in a puff of smoke.

To complement the radio, I cleverly started a Facebook group page called Bermondsey radio and invited my friends initially to join the radio community. The response was unbelievable, imagine everyone is trapped in their homes and needed entertaining. I was the man. I had the music and the dulcet tones, and because I had no work for the forceable future I was going to help my community out with the only way I knew I could, with music.

I saw others try their best by doing live you tube DJ sets, I found it to be hilarious, and they didn't last long, think about it, who wants to see a DJ's beer belly while listening to "Follow me" by Aly-us? I knew Bermondsey radio was onto a winner when we had four thousand Facebook friends in our group. There was no way I was going to go visual; we would have lost all our listeners if they had seen me close up, believe you me. Radio is such a powerful media, it's still here, even with the developments of hd tv and the number of channels that are available these days. Use your imagination when you listen to the radio and it is truly fantastic, and I presented the shows in a very informal way at times, and sometimes we had to present in a very sobering way. But that is the point, you the listener went with it, and you enjoyed the ride. It could be sad, happy, hilarious, informative all in sixty minutes, and you wanted more.

Soon there was many ways to tune into Bermondsey radio, Radioline is a popular way but would sometimes lose signal, going straight to Radio king website and searching for Bermondsey Radio is the best, so too is our free app on android, and available on the play store. This app has several benefits including receiving a text when we are next broadcasting. When I say we, I mean we, Bermondsey radio cannot function without our Admin, they are integral to the daily running of the station and they help in many ways, I have no idea how we picked our admin, but I do remember I kept adding them. We had nearly twenty at one point. In no particular order.........

Wendy Fitzgerald has been with us since day one and I will always remember her enthusiasm and excitement, just the thought of having her very own radio station. Her favourite song is Street life by the Crusaders, and I always play the twelve-inch version as Wendy does like a twelve incher! She is a member of the Throb mob and is a very good vocalist, I remixed one of her tracks "Ernie, the fastest milkman in the west", a duet with Benny hill, and he's brown bread!

Along with her husband Martin, they are proud sponsors of BR and both like to tune in on a Sunday for some easy listening tunes.

Colette Savage is so very kind, I can't even begin to tell you how much she means to BR and I don't wish to embarrass her, so I won't. She lives in Scotland with her family and loves Ska music particularly the beat, they had hits with "Mirror in the bathroom" and "Hands off she's mine", she also likes Paul Weller and has great taste in music, she has won the "quiz at noon" many times, and has stuck with us from the very beginning. I will spare her blushes and not tell you of all the generous thing she has done for Bermondsey Radio.

Keely Brown is married to Bluey very happily for 28 years and has also been with BR since the beginning, she loves Light of the world and often asks for "Sunny" by Bobby Hebb as her son is named Sonny. Keely is a very talented poet as you will see later in the book, she is also into amateur dramatics, and she is the Throb Mother...more about that later.

Carly Britton is married and got three lovely children, she always gets what she wants when it comes to requests on BR, and she has a heart of gold, always putting others before herself. She has also won the Quiz at noon many times, but she is a bad loser, if she loses to a technicality, I don't hear the last of it. Apart from that she is an angel.

Beckie Fox and her son **Jonnie Fox** are part of the furniture on BR, always requesting songs on Sunday morning, and if there any seconds on the requests, you can always rely on these two to come up with some great tunes. Bermondsey radio could not survive without these two legends. "This next song is for Beckie Beckie, Beckie, Beckie, Beckie Fox".

Clare Pascoe has helped Bermondsey radio so much it is unbelievable, she is always promoting us on Facebook and we would be lost without her, she loves Soul music and her favourite song is "Extraordinary girl" by the O Jays, Another one that has won the Quiz many times, she always comments on everything we do, and I love seeing people taking part in the radio show, I love it.

Claire Rayner has been with us all the way through and takes part in everything we do, another great Quiz person, she has won it loads of times. And with her man Dazzo Millwall Markham have contributed to the success of Bermondsey radio by requesting some fantastic songs along this journey, including Sydney Youngblood and Otis Redding.

Emma bowers has always been my favourite admin, very helpful and always telling me what to do, and giving me fresh ideas, in the early days she was addicted to Bermondsey radio and all the great music we played. She loves to hear "O-o-h child" by the five stairsteps and when she requests it, it would be duly played.

Darren Chandler is not only a top admin but also presents BR's rock show "Lockstock and one Darren Chandler" it went down a storm and attracted many listeners, but unfortunately sent me into a nervous breakdown, I spent more time downloading songs for the show than I did for my own, so we had to call it a day. Darren is a big Millwall fan and loves his Pie and mash, Paul Weller, Madness, Billy Joel, and the Boss are his favourite's.

Yvette Chandler loves soul music, Teena Marie, George Benson and the Band AKA she helps Bermondsey radio beyond belief and always listens in when she can, one of the first to join the Facebook group page she helped BR with her kindness and her generosity.

Julie Ann Gifford has contributed to Bermondsey radio by out bidding everyone else to get an Awning for her house, installed by Simon and Jimmy at Millreef signs, her generosity knows no bounds, and Bermondsey radio could have gone down the plug hole without her help at that time. When we presented a country show Julie would request "Tennessee Whiskey" by Chris Stapleton.

Katy Hansen loved Bermondsey radio and would request many songs, she loves soul music and dance stuff and contributed to the promotion of the station in her own way and was much appreciated.

Kerrie Pooke is sex mad; she has sex on the brain morning noon and night, and that is no exaggeration. I have no idea what other hobbies she has, but it certainly is not Bermondsey radio. But if it was not for Kerrie Pooke, I would not have a job right now, she helped me in designing my CV and along with Colette Savage got me the fantastic job I have in Westminster today.

My Admin for Bermondsey radio has seen everything, and have heard everything, they have different personalities, we have ups and downs, but they all have one thing in common, and that is loyalty. In various ways, they have done their best to help Bermondsey radio. And I will always be forever grateful to each and every one of them.

Initially Bermondsey radio was providing a service, remember everyone in March was under lockdown rules. People were trapped inside their flats, we had a very captive audience, and they needed entertaining. I had to venture out to buy essentials, I would walk down to my local Tesco's to get essential groceries, water, milk and bread. Sometimes I would go down to Southwark Park Road to the bakers and get a pastie and a couple of donuts. It was round this time I had a serious health scare myself, on a walk down to Tesco's at Abbey Street, I had to stop after just a few yards, maybe seventy or a hundred, I was breathless, I felt I was eighty years old; I couldn't put another foot forward, I was knackered. I sat on a nearby wall, blimey Had I caught covid19? I made it to Tesco's and back and dropped the bags of shopping inside my front door, stumbled to my bedroom and collapsed on the bed, gasping for air. After ten minutes I felt a bit better and asked for advice over the internet from my admin, they told me to ring 911 and describe my symptoms. I spoke to a nurse who told me to drink water with honey and lemon juice, loads of it, she said it would cleanse my lungs, I ordered it off amazon and expected the delivery the next day. I was in trouble there for a while. I remember when I did my usual broadcast the listeners could hear me gasping for air when I was introducing the songs and asked me where I lived, Judith Bond was the first to arrive with essential bags of shopping, I heard a bang on my door knocker and by the time I got to the door there was bags of shopping, and Judith had scarpered. I was out of breath just getting to the door. The amazon delivery arrived, honey, lemon juice and I already had bottles of water, delivered by Iceland's. After a few days of taking lemon and honey in large quantities I did start to feel a lot better, my breathing improved gradually and then My admin let me know they were coming up in the morning, but wouldn't say why, this set me into a very anxious mode, I was nervous they intended to enter my flat and see the mess and rubbish all around me. I needn't have worried, they arrived with bags and bags of groceries, it was incredible. I didn't ask for this, but they heard my breathing during the radio shows and acted. My admin is something special. This was not the last time they would surprise me.

I was doing a radio show on a Saturday night when we began, it was a disco night, and our listeners were listening with the rest of their family, who were miles apart, but they were requesting songs for each other. We were playing Phil Fearon & Galaxy and Dancing tight, the real thing and You to me are everything, these listeners were requesting some dance classics and that is why the station was a success.

In this first lockdown unfortunately, we had friends that died of Covid19, we helped the families grieve by letting them use our platform to get the news out there, Larry a DJ from the Stanley pub passed away and the response on BR was phenomenal, we did a special show for him, and lots of his friends listened and participated, we did what we could for our community and I think the family were comforted by our show. We didn't hear anything, but we carried on doing what we thought to be right.

Terry Coakley passed away at a very young age and once again BR did all we could to ease the pain of the family in such sad times. The funeral directors Albins were under government guidelines and only a few mourners could attend the service, so once again we allowed the mourners to use our platform and I played appropriate music during the wake. This was a very tragic occasion, because of the age of Terry and his lovely girlfriend Amy and the family appreciated our efforts at BR. In those early months of the lockdown, it was shocking, many of my friends were on ventilators and it was touch and go with a few of them.

My savings were rapidly running out, and there was no sign of the lockdown being lifted, in fact it was getting worse. No chance of work and one of my Admin Wendy had an idea. She suggested a Facebook fundraiser, I was unsure at first, but as my funds dwindled, I decided to give it a go. I set a goal of £1000 to see how things went, and I was shocked at the initial response. It was barmy because people I didn't even know were parting with donations and friends, I had known all my life didn't flinch and ignored my plight, but I thought to myself, they were in even bigger poo than I was, they must have been, or why are they not helping me? In one week, we raised the target, but now we couldn't rest on the generosity of our listeners, we had to think of other ways of raising funds to help me and Bermondsey radio survive.

Just to let you know, there are a few sayings in the very strange world of BR, so there is the first one, BR obviously means Bermondsey radio. Next one I use it quite a lot when everything is ok and running smoothly and that is Tickety boo, you will hear me say this all the time, because generally speaking, everything is fine. Round about twelve noon on Sunday I get in a right tangle, because I have so much to do at that time, namely the Quiz at noon, that is when you hear me say "I am in a right Mucking fuddle" translated it mean fucking muddle, hope that didn't offend you too much. At BR we love to use cockney rhyming slang, we love to confuse the old Bill. When I am having a swift Scotch and coke, you will normally hear me say " I don't half fancy a gold watch!"(Scotch) I will let you know if I think of any more.

Let me explain how this radio malarky works, it is straight forward, I am sitting in my flat on the Dickens estate and on my laptop, I have a lapel mic connected to the usb socket and headphones connected to the headphone socket, and I put these on me earholes to listen to what I am broadcasting. I use a software called Virtual DJ to connect to Radio king, who provide me with a "Server" that sends my signal to anyone who connects to Bermondsey radio, on bad days we get nuked by the Russians, and it takes me a few seconds to get us back on air, those Russians get right on my tits, there is no need for it, I hate the Basterds. We have jingles we play on Bermondsey radio, I love playing jingles, it gives the station a real feel of being a proper radio station. My favourite jingle goes something like this "No one likes us we don't care, but we love the music on Bermondsey radio" got a Millwall feel about it.

Bermondsey radio have our very own sponsors, without whom we would all be doomed. And our main sponsor is "Stansfeld football club" who sponsors all shows on Bermondsey radio and has a "Match of the day" soundtrack. The team is based in Chislehurst and play at the Glebe sports ground in Foxbury avenue, Chislehurst. They originate from Bermondsey and their chairman is Mr Ian Rooney, who has been fully behind BR from the beginning. They play in the SCEFL, and we thank Ian for his continued support.

Within each Super Sunday show we have a quiz at noon, this normally takes place at midday, followed by requests from you, our listeners, and the Birthday shout outs for the forth-coming week ahead is at 1pm sharp on a Super Sunday afternoon.

Let me explain the Quiz at noon, when we first tried the quiz there was murders, it was really competitive, our admin used to fight amongst themselves, it is hilarious, do you know what I love about BR ? it's the taking part, I want you to request a song, enter the quiz, and have a shout out at 1pm, that is all I ask, and I will be a happy DJ. Remember listeners always take part, you will love it. I promise. So many funny things have happened during the Quiz, the funniest moment was when, one afternoon, David Cook took part, and the rest is BR history, let me explain…….

When we broadcasted seven days a week we had a Quiz every day, you could take part only if you were a member of our Facebook group and had to "like" the Quiz thread in the room. I would play three songs and you would need to name the three artists and name the three songs. The winner needed six out of six to win a virtual trophy in the room and three songs of their choice to be played next day in the next Quiz at noon, essentially you need to type the six answers as quick as possible and quickly look at your typing, for errors, press the enter button and hope you were first past the post with all six correct. The three songs are normally very easy. I do accept a spelling error, or two, but a completely wrong word will be disqualified. In the early days this quiz was so competitive there would be stewards enquiries into almost every quiz. My admin was very passionate about the quiz and wanted the coveted prize of the three songs! David Cook loved to take part, and as I always say, "take part in BR and you will always get more out of it" The three songs I played this day was Fairground – Simply red, Up the junction – Squeeze and Copacabana – Barry Manilow. I have no idea who won the quiz on this day because what followed was a classic golden moment that we all will never forget. After checking a few correct contestants live over the air I now stare at David Cook's answers, by the way David is better known as Cookie, and you will never meet a nicer person we all love him, and he has a reputation of cracking us up with laughter, at the way he replies to the quiz. I am looking at my mobile device, focusing on his spelling, he has a habit of making the odd mistake. Oh my god, I read it outlive on air "And Cookie has put Copacabana by Batty Manilow!" well I lost it, I started giggling at first, then it became uncontrollable raucous belly laughs, and every time I repeated the line it made me worse. I tried to get on with the show, but when the next song finished, I was still laughing.

Cookie let me thank you for creating one of the great memories of BR, you just couldn't make it up, could you? I hope my writing has given it justice; it was pure comedy genius.

We had some fantastic personalities join us at BR and I will try and mention as many as possible because they made listening to Bermondsey radio an absolute dream. The Legend Jackie O'Brien and her mate Jan Perkins loved picking songs for me to play. The Pina colada song by Rupert Holmes became the most requested song on BR due to them. Jackie loves BR, she can have her songs played and have her name announced and all her family and friends would be listening out for her shout out. Jackie uses fruity language occasionally, well, quiet a lot actually. She tends to use the word "James Hunt" (cockney rhyming slang) rather a lot, and us folk on BR are not used to hearing this word in a sentence, well not as frequently as "The Legend" uses it. Once she called into the show live, I stupidly put her on air! The airwaves turned blue, with James Hunt here, James Hunt there, James Hunt every fudging where. She said, "Are you fudging well going to let Paddy sing a song or what?" I submitted to her request, like I always do, and asked her to "pass the phone to Paddy before we get thrown off air!" "What? I aint said nothing!" she said innocently. As she passed the phone to Paddy. "Oh Danny Boy" rang out across Bermondsey radio, he sang it perfectly in tune and remembered all the words and entertained us royally. Shani Murphy is Jackie's beautiful daughter and has a heart of gold, she never swears, unlike her mum. Jan Perkins, I worked with in the Ship, St Marys church street, she was the glamorous barmaid, and I was the DJ, we had some fun in that pub when Del Boy had it, and the parties were great on Sunday afternoons. Jan also works over near Claridge's in the heart of the West end. Er I think it's called Little Molton street, yes, I'm sure it is. Jan likes Ronan Keating "Life is a rollercoaster" I remember, but her mood changes her choice almost daily. The Legend that is Jackie O'Brien has a heart of gold too, she cooked me Christmas dinner with all the trimmings and she dropped it off to me with Shani driving the car on Christmas day 2020, an act of kindness that I shall never forget, I think I still have the massive dinner plate here in my cupboard, I must get it back to her, she delivered Christmas dinner with pigs in blankets, and afters, Christmas crackers, yes, on Christmas day! That's why Jackie O'Brien is a Legend. Hold on a minute Jan Perkins, I've got it, It's South Molton Street innit!

We had a rock show on Bermondsey radio, hosted by Darren Chandler and assisted by Jimmy Deller. It was a technical nightmare to get on air, they were in Eltham, and I would press all the buttons and faders in Bermondsey. It was not quite as simple as that. The show was called "Lockstock and one Darren chandler" and it was presented well, with Darren's great knowledge of the rock scene and choices of rock classics was very appealing and would attract many listeners. The only reason we had to stop was the time it took me to download the tracks and then try to find them on my computer, it took hours, and it was just too much for me in the end. What fun we had on those shows, and the listeners got into it. Like all BR radio shows, Darren's rock show can be listened to on my Soundcloud account just search "Bermondseysnumberone" hopefully one day we could bring the Rock show back, if we played songs already in my music library, but it would compromise the quality of the music, because there is no way I am downloading music files for hours on end again. Darren is very enthusiastic and helps Bermondsey radio when he can, he came up with some great questions for the group page, and always got our listeners thinking. In the early days Darren would win the Quiz at noon all the time, and there was controversy when he misspelt Jamiroquai and failed to win the Supreme champion title, after prompting from my admin he was awarded the title because he really deserved it. When he sits back and just listens to the broadcast he is missed, and when he gets involved BR is a much better place. Specially his arguments with the admin team, there was always a standoff, as nobody would back down. But it was all done in fun and jest, nobody really meant it. Did they?

I have bad memories of the lockdown in particular my barnet! As the lockdown got longer, so did my hair. When I would pop out to the shops to get a dozen toilet rolls, the cashier in Tesco's thought I was prehistoric man. One of the shop assistants said, "You don't arf look like Shaggy off Scooby Doo" So when the lockdown was over, I was gagging to get a trim. So, I went down to Jimmy's hairdressers at Spenlow house and was greeted with a que a mile long! I had to make an appointment! Ah well, another day looking like Gilbert O'Sullivan. Next morning, I was in the chair and twenty minutes later I was trimmed, neat, and tidy again, it felt so good. Best score I've ever spent.

CHAPTER THIRTEEN

SAD TIMES & HAPPY TIMES

If you look back to the beginning of this book, when I drove my van for the first time after I passed my test. I collided into a brand-new van coming out of the Ford dealership in Blue Anchor Lane. The gentleman who came to my rescue was Freddie Collins, he took control of the situation, and calmed everyone down. Unfortunately, during lockdown Freddie passed away and I presented a special wake in his memory. Fred was a lovely man, he worked for Albins I knew him for fifty years, when I was a youngster I knew his son Paul, who unfortunately died at a young age, and Paul was a great footballer, playing for Fisher and Welling. The funeral restrictions were still in place, so once again Bermondsey radio did its duty, and helped its community in its hour of need. We did this time and again throughout this terrible time, we were resilient and determined, Covid19 was not going to beat Bermondsey radio.

Simon Steers and Jimmy Shilling were one of Bermondsey radio's top sponsors, they were the guvnor's of Millreef signs, they came up with a great idea to help Bermondsey radio, they offered a free awning for me to auction live on the radio, with the money going to keep BR on air. These two lads are the best at what they do, and this act of generosity was just what BR needed, we were running out of funds, and this was a fantastic thing to do to help BR. The auction was advertised, and the bids started coming in. Right from the very beginning it was clear who was going to get this brilliant awning. Julie Ann Gifford was on a mission and when Sunday came around, she did the most generous thing I have ever seen. I wouldn't have believed it if I hadn't seen it with my own eyes. Nobody else made a bid but Julie kept bidding, and bidding. I closed the bidding, and the winning bid was surprise surprise by Julie Ann Gifford, at £750! WOW! That is a person with a very big heart and has helped BR beyond belief. And what about Millreef signs, they donated there awning free of charge and installed it for free. Julie Ann Gifford made a bid that she didn't have to do, this, right here, was the Bermondsey spirit.

The first sponsor for Bermondsey radio was "Nellie's Flowers" by Sharon Rooney, her arranging is legendary, and she only buys the best flowers at convent garden in Vauxhall. Sharon's husband is the Director of Stansfeld football club Ian Rooney, and they too have an advert on BR, If you order flowers from Sharon you will not be disappointed, she is based in Eltham and gets orders from all over southeast London.

Meanwhile Bermondsey radio was going from strength to strength and the Facebook group had over four thousand members. The thing is, where were they? one of the big mysteries was, we have loads of members, but it was always the same people taking part in the shows and donating to the station. This used to wind me up. But these days I just accept it, it is what it is, if they don't want to donate or take part, that is up to them. But if you are reading this book, please take part.

Steve Chandler and his wife Georgie have supported Bermondsey radio since the beginning and have contributed to helping BR when they can afford to. They helped when we had the "Toy drive" and helped kids in Bermondsey get a Christmas present with the help of Kathy Heather from "Love north Southwark" Bermondsey radio helped over one hundred families recieve toys to open on Christmas day, and that is something that I am very proud of. Steve is a real character and I remember he requested a band called black grape and a song called Reverend, we had so many complaints about that song it was incredible. "What the f**k is this load of shite?" It got hammered, the admin went into one. We had to take it off air, my admin are very strict and this was the only time I had to take the song off, Steve took it well, and give credit where its due, it was Steve's idea to award winners of the Quiz at noon with three songs as a prize and I thank Georgie and Steve for helping BR in those early days.

Nicky B, AKA Nicky Beyzade is another kind-hearted young lady that helped BR and went through a lot of hassle due to the government's guidelines during the lockdowns. She is one of our sponsors with her business "Browse & Beauty by Nicky B" She has been resilient and is now bouncing back very strongly. Nicky has a lovely bubbly personality and has a very generous nature. Do you remember when she presented her own show on BR, she was brilliant, lots of great music and dedications to her family and friends. She is so generous that if she got a new customer through BR she would send me an extra tenner, what a lovely lady. Nicky B was also our weather lady when BR was on seven days a week, I think she enjoyed doing that, and she was very good at it. She would request a song and take part in the quiz; she is brilliant for Bermondsey radio, and I thank her from the bottom of my heart.

In the early days of BR, I played in the morning till about 2pm I can only tell you it was a great show of fantastic music, and these songs took over the end of the show. That's what friends are for by Dionne Warwick, Heal the world by Michael Jackson and we'll meet again by Dame Vera Lynne. There were other songs, but these three stood out. The emotions floating about was evident in the song choices, when will I see you again by the Chi-lites and miss you like crazy by Natalie Cole. These songs were also played a lot on BR.
Then we had Captain Tom Moore, who was knighted by the Queen before he died, and raised £39 million, he also had a number one single with Michael Ball and met the footballer, David Beckham. We could play patriotic songs like no other radio station and when Captain Tom sadly passed away, Bermondsey radio did a special show for Sir Tom Moore, lots of Vera Lynn was played on that day, and shortly after, the nation mourned a national treasure, Dame Vera's passing.

We remembered VE day, and of course remembrance Sunday, yes if I had to sum up that period there was a lot of patriotic music being played at that time, come to think about it we also had the death of the Prince of Edinburgh, the longest serving consort in history. Her Majesty misses him so much, and she just recently celebrated seventy years as our monarch, I am honoured to have played music for those occasions, I am a very proud to have played music for those lives. It is an honour and a privilege.

At this time, I was helped by Karen Supple and Kevin Morley, they helped Bermondsey radio in so many ways, donating to help keep Bermondsey radio on air, in return, I presented a virtual party for them on a few special occasions. There is nothing like a virtual party, its personalised to the music you want to hear, I remember Karen would Bluetooth BR to her jukebox and then blast it out through the house, a great sound system for a great radio station. It was near Christmas, and they delivered a fantastic hamper to me when I had nothing. The kindness and generosity of these listeners was incredible. I would like to thank Karen and Kevin for helping me in such dark times, I will never forget your kindness.

The Virtual parties really took off because everyone was trapped indoors, if it was your 40th birthday you could celebrate together online with all the family and friends virtually "together" all in one place, on BR. Every Saturday night there was a special party with dance songs played till eleven o'clock. Hundreds would tune in and dance, it was crazy. I presented all sorts of music genre's, Country, Cheese, Reggae, songs from Theatre, and loads more. Our virtual football show featured all Millwall's games and one hour before kick-off it would be Status quo and Rockin all over the world, Wonderwall, Hey Jude, let em come, and many more football songs, it proved very popular as, at that time fans were not allowed in the stadiums to watch the mighty lions. I did all their games home and away, and all England's games in the Euro's, Three Lions, back home, world in motion, it was great playing all the footie songs, Bermondsey radio can get away with it. My admin would suggest a show and we would give it a go, always having a notice board in the Facebook group page, so listeners could pick their favourite song. This is the key to why Bermondsey radio was very popular, I played your song and also get a shout out to all your family and friends, it has been the winning formula right from the very start, and as I write this book it's the same formula today. I only broadcast Sunday's these days 10.30am till 7pm and on average get five to six hundred listeners, that's not bad, Covid19 has slivered into the background, hopefully forever, and to have hundreds still tuning in is amazing. But if you like easy listening music on a Sunday morning you now know where to come.

Now that I have a proper job again there is no need to donate to keep BR on air, it's my turn to pay for all that, but all donations received, this year will go to Love North Southwark, a local charity that helped me get through the pandemic and live to tell the tail. Last Christmas we collected brand new toys to be distributed to families that have hit hard times, local families, their children opened a Christmas gift from our wonderful listeners, over one hundred families in Southwark had a happier Christmas because of us. This Christmas will be even better for our kids, we have an appeal running right now on BR as I write this, and ALL donations to BR will go to Love North Southwark and the lady that runs it, with her wonderful volunteers is Kathy Heather. If you would like to donate for our Bermondsey kids, drop your brand-new toy in at Slippers place, Southwark Park rd., or simply donate to Bermondsey radio and it will find its way there. Thank you in advance.

During the pandemic I was to say the least, financially challenged. Help came via donations and during this time I was approached by Kathy Heather to promote her food bank on the radio, which I did, and she was very grateful. The plug on BR encouraged people to pop in and get some groceries in their shopping bags, 15 items, for a fiver, all sorts of essential items Milk, veg, meat, pasta, etc. etc.. It came to a point where I had to ask for help from her, yes Bermondsey's number one DJ was asking for help. I had to swallow my pride and realise I was in trouble. Kathy was brilliant, she herself, would deliver to my door twice a week and sometimes Rachel Bentley with all sorts of goodies. Therefore, it's important to pay back the people that helped me through this nightmare, and the TOY DRIVE is part of it. Please donate and help us provide local kids with a present to open this Christmas. Part of the money from the sale of this paperback or Kindle will go to TOY DRIVE, so tell your friends buy it and increase the funds to get more presents. Last year Bermondsey radio collected over 100 new toys to distribute to less fortunate children in the Bermondsey area. Let's see if we can do better this year for local kids. Thank you.

When we were allowed to, and the restrictions were lifted, BR had a social gathering and raffle at the best pub in Bermondsey, run by Micky and Pat Jarman, the Ship aground is right next door to the fire station that was used in the tv series London's burning. It's now a very modern fire station, and occasionally the sirens will go off and the fire engines will emerge and race to their next emergency.

The pub game was in limbo at that time, not knowing when they would be able to open their doors again. The ship aground is one of the few real pubs left in the area, run by local people, Pat and Mick, they know, and cater for their customers very well, because they know the Bermondsey people very well. This was the perfect venue for BR because the radio station was formed to help our local community, and all the regular customers realised that BR was succeeding. The support we had on that day was unbelievable, apart from the regulars returning, they were joined by BR listeners, loads of them. The BR admin team was there in force and Clare Pascoe and Beckie fox helped in selling raffle tickets. Raffle prizes were donated by so many people, on the day we raised a few hundred pounds to keep Bermondsey radio on air.

There were some fantastic prizes up for grabs, donated by our sponsors, and Pat and Mick contributed generously too with twelve-year-old whiskeys and speciality Gins. This day was a great success and the generosity of the people there was incredible. The compliments I received about BR and how it had helped so many people were the highlight for me, and this is what the people were saying to me "Noel, you really don't realise how much you have done to help me through this pandemic". And I would reply "I did my best, I helped you, and you helped me".

One young lad, the son of Beckie Fox, took the microphone, Jonnie Fox was his name and for such a young age, said a few words that brought a tear to my eye, and this is what he said "I would just like to thank Bermondsey radio for getting us through these hard times"

It was followed by a loud cheer of approval and massive round of applause from the crowd that attended this special event. Listeners travelled from all over the country to be there. David Cook and his girlfriend Tara Hudson travelled up from the south coast, Trudi P. Hart came up from Cambridge. There was a big crowd all with positive vibes, and just glad to be out in a pub again. Mind you, there was still a few covid rules in place, but I was just happy to be amongst people again, it had been such a long time for me. The last time I was in the company of so many people, was when I was on holiday in Goa back in February 2020. I never dreamed this would happen to the world. But we made it out of the other side, by helping each other. I think we did a very good job of it, something to be proud of.

The Rooney family are a big part of why Bermondsey radio survived. Sharon was the first sponsor on Bermondsey radio with "Nellie's flowers", her Bespoke florist based in Eltham. Ian was a big fan of the music and was behind us all the way along with their children, Luke, and Abbie. They all consistently donated to BR, and when it was Ian's birthday, he insisted on having a virtual party and instructed his virtual guests to donate to help BR survive. When the day came, we had many listeners from all over, including in Ireland, the UK, and even in New York city. We had so many requests that day and loads of donations from people I hadn't seen or heard of since I was a young boy. Richard Crawley otherwise known as Dogsie donated. As kids I would see him often, as he lived near the Gregorian pub, across the road from me. These days I sometimes text him and chat about his nephew Zak, who opens the batting for the England cricket team. Tim Collins donated, a very successful businessman, who now lives in Ireland and played for the Fisher. And if we go back to 1969 Tim, as a young boy, and his family moved out of 19 Rudge house on the Dickens estate and my family moved in.

The music on this virtual birthday party was superb, chosen by Ian's virtual guests, who were listening from all around the globe. We raised a lot of money, due to the kindness and generosity of Ian, he always says to me "Noel, that was a great day, wasn't it?" I must agree with him, like everything to do with Bermondsey radio, everything seems to fall into place, like it was meant to be. Now it's the same with writing this book, I haven't written since my school days, yet it all seems to be falling into place again.

It was Ian's idea to organise a raffle to raise funds for BR and it worked. He even helped by selling raffle tickets at a Stansfeld FC home fixture, Ian is the Chairman of Stansfeld, and they sponsor all shows on Bermondsey radio, they won the league last season and were promoted and are now in the same league as Fisher, the Southern counties football east. I do enjoy non-league football these days and my allegiance is now firmly with Stansfeld, they play at the Glebe sports ground in Chislehurst but make no mistake their roots are in Bermondsey.

We had some very sad times during this pandemic and when my good friend Danny Herd lost his mum Carole, this affected me personally as I have always had connections with the Herd family, Danny's father Joe, and Carole ran the Fisher club bar and asked me to play music there on a regular basis. They are now together in heaven, but when they were with us, they were the nicest of people to me, when I was working with Dockhead cars I would take my tea break at the Servewell café in West Lane, just off Jamaica rd. And meet up with Joe and Yos Arif, oh my god what a double act these two were, they would take the right piss out of me (in a good way), I can still remember the laughter, they both had wonderful infectious laughs, I loved their company, and I miss them both dearly. Carole was a lady, and her kids are a credit to her, the way she brought them up. Young Joe was a fantastic goalkeeper and played for the Fisher, Kelly is a beautiful person with a wonderful smile, like her mum. Danny is a great guy along with his wife Karen have been very good to me, it's a friendship that will always be there, they are good people.

When the day came, the day of the funeral, we arranged to start the broadcast when they had all arrived back home, Danny was going to text me when they got back. Can you imagine the responsibility? What an honour, and the trust they put in me. And as if by magic, the emotional songs began. I do not plan anything, I never do, it just seems to fall into place. Hundreds were listening at every syllable that I said. "Fly me to the moon" was requested by Danny and that set the mood, classy music for a classy lady, then we had requests from all the family and friends and before we knew it, we were playing party songs enabling the mourners to dance and enjoy the night, just as Carole would have wanted. The music went long into the night, and even though they were all apart, Bermondsey radio made it seem as though they were all together. It was a tremendous tribute with a lot of emotion. I was privileged and honoured to play music for a wonderful lady and a great family. Thank you for asking me.

We would broadcast seven days a week at this time, each day starting the early morning show at 10.30am with all the features, your requests, Quiz at noon, birthday shout outs and at 10am we had the weather report for the day by Nicky B, who was our kind and generous sponsor of BR with her business Browse & Beauty with Nicky B. Nicky once had a go of her own show, and she was very good at it. She said to me afterwards "I really enjoyed that Noel" One day we might let her have another go, we will save it for a special day. Thursday nights on BR we would alternate the music genre, it would be from 7pm till 10pm, and would be a country show or a reggae show mostly, and they would prove very popular. Carly Britton once suggested a Abba/Beatles show, and it worked very well, it is available on my sound cloud account, along with other shows and mixes. Keely Brown presented on BR, a one-off show, with lots of her friends and family listening, she took to it, like a duck to water. Keely Brown has a wonderful talent and that is poetry she has brightened up our days with some excellent poems during these sad times, towards the end of the book we will publish another gem from Keely.

As BR developed and we knew we were going to be in this for the long haul, Bermondsey radio dug its heels in and was prepared for the months ahead. Boris was very ill himself with the virus and the restrictions would be altered almost weekly, when is this covid19 nightmare going to end?

We would see familiar listeners coming back repeatedly. Some of these became addicted to the station, needing their daily fix of BR, they could rely on us. Every day when I published the Facebook notice board in our group page there would be a race to get your name up first. It was always between Jaq Hull, Carly Britton, and Claire Rayner.

On a good day we would get around twenty requests per show, and then if we had time I would announce "If you would like a second song, please go to the notice board and jot it down". Yes, seconds is popular I must admit. These days on BR we broadcast just on a Sunday from 10.30am till 7pm, it goes something like this 10.30am till 2.00pm Super Sunday, 2.00pm till 2.30pm The Chart show (latest chart top ten) 2.30pm till 3.30pm Top of the Pops (from a particular year) and at 3.30pm Super Sunday will be repeated, and we would end that day's broadcast at 7.00pm. We will stick to this formula for the forceable future.

I do like to make the show about the music, I usually start the show with tracks that I have chosen, but once the Quiz at noon has found its new champion, we begin playing the requests, chosen by our listeners. If BR didn't get requests, the show would be flat, and there would be no point in us presenting a show. The whole point is, get the listeners involved, whether they request a song, take part in the Quiz, or have a shout out on the station, they must take part.

If you like a good laugh and need cheering up, then tune in at noon on a Sunday morning. Bermondsey radio isn't Bermondsey radio without mistakes, booboo's, clangers, and it always seem to happen at twelve noon. It's because I am trying to juggle so many things at the same time, while presenting a radio show. In front of me I have my laptop with virtual DJ running, Facebook with the group page running, messenger, WhatsApp, the virtual trophy (about to be published with the winner's name), and my smart phone by my side. (That makes a beep when someone messages me). So, you can see it a time bomb waiting to go off, and it often does. Just one thing can interrupt my concentration and Boom! I get myself in a right mucking fuddle!

There are some people that have helped Bermondsey radio beyond the call of duty, and Bermondsey radio had our very own Charlie's Angels, and they were Lee Ellis, Nicki Whiting, and Luisa Hutchins. They, along with their family and friends helped keep Bermondsey

164

radio on air with unbelievable generosity. They booked me for so many virtual parties it was unbelievable, and the thing was, they picked the most fantastic music, so they were the dream team. Can I say to these three ladies in particular you lifted me up, when I was down, you saved Bermondsey radio on many occasions with your generosity. And I will never forget what you did as long as I live. Thank you from the bottom of my heart.

When Lee and Luisa went away on holiday together, when the flying restrictions were lifted, they would tune in and request a song from wherever they were. For example, if they were in Ibiza, I would say they were in Rhodes! And if they were in Marbella, I would say they were in Benidorm! It was a little joke I loved to play with them. They would be around the pool listening on the hotels wi-fi and get all excited when they realised their song was about to be played. When I announced over the airways "This next song is for Lee Ellis and Luisa Hutchins, they would like to hear Was that all it was by Jean Carne, they are enjoying the sun in Corfu!" well, I could hear the laughter from the two ladies back in Bermondsey, they, of course, were in a totally different place, but that was the point, take part in Bermondsey radio and you will be rewarded with music and laughter, not bad eh?

We had a motto on our posters that would adorn our Facebook group page "Stay in, cheer up, and dance" we were trapped indoors and when we were allowed outside, masks had to be worn. Especially in confined places. I knew many of my friends who ended up on ventilators, some escaped with long covid, some lost their fight and passed away. I have had all the jabs, I have had covid19, but the jabs helped me with the effect it had on my body. Testing positive, and I thought I had just a summer cold, so the jabs have worked so far. Stay in with your loved ones, cheer up, don't get depressed, and dance round the kitchen table and enjoy yourself. That is what the motto meant to me and my listeners, and it was at the top of all the posters we put on the group page. Saturday night fever was obviously a Saturday night show, and we played disco music to dance to, listeners requested all sorts of tunes, CeCe Peniston, Robin S, Sybil, Jocelyn Brown, it was brilliant they were staying in, cheering up, and dancing their little socks off.

Back in March 2020 the lockdown was implemented, Bermondsey radio began with just five listeners, Jean Barry and Dave London were the first, and they listened in from Tenerife where they lived. I had previously played at their wedding reception just off the Walworth Road, it was a fantastic party, with lots of dancing and drinking. When I broadcast for the first time they were there, texting me, telling me that they could hear me loud and clear. Lee Ellis was there on that first day and requested some great soul music like Glow of love by Change and Jean Carne and a song called Was that all it was. Sharon Saunders listened in and loved to request her favourite songs from John Holt and Amy Winehouse. Wendy Fitzgerald joined us on that first broadcast and loved to hear We are family by Sister Sledge and Street life by the Crusaders. From five on the first day, we now have around five hundred listeners on a Super Sunday. That is not bad considering, at time of writing, the country is almost back to normal. Why are they still tuned in when they could be out in the sunshine enjoying life? It must be the music, the requests, and the pure fact that it is their station, always will be.

When we started, we just had music, then came the mic, we could now introduce songs properly. We added sponsors with their own adverts, and our very own station Id's. The ability to record the shows and put them up on Sound cloud came later-on, and I wish I had figured it out earlier, because we missed out on some classic moments on BR by not recording them. Eddie Webber kindly did an interview on BR by phoning in and talking about the projects he was working on, he also told us about his book about his life in tv and the movies, you must check it out it's called Hi-diddle-di-de: from the streets of Bermondsey to lights, camera, action! Eddie and I was good mates at St

Joseph's school in George row Bermondsey. As I write this book, he is playing a character in Eastenders called Dodge, an old acquaintance of Phil Mitchell, so we wish him all the best with that role. Yes so, I wish I had recorded this interview, Eddie was very entertaining, maybe we will do another one in the future if Eddie fancies it.

We also presented a show dedicated to Barry Albin Dyer, who was the most famous undertaker in the UK, it was the anniversary of his passing, 6th June 2015, and it was a natural thing to do, he loved Bermondsey, and we loved him. I had previously played the music at Barry's 60th birthday party and played music for his son Jon on several occasions. Barry was so loved by the people of Bermondsey that when I heard it was his anniversary, we dedicated the show to him. I think it was Ian Rooney who phoned Jon and told him that we were dedicating the show to their father, in the middle of show the phone rang and it was Jon, oh my god, I made a quick decision, I was going to put him live on air! Jon and his brother Simon are the ultimate professionals, and they have carried on the work of Albins, just how their father would have wanted. Jon spoke of how kind it was for Bermondsey radio to dedicate this show for his father and the family were all very moved by our actions. My reply to Jon was "Your father had helped so many people in this area, and was loved and respected by our whole community, this is our time to show your family how much we really care, so thank you Jon and your brother Simon, keep up the fantastic work you are doing in this pandemic and thank you for coming on air to speak to us in these dark times" Jon thanked me graciously, and I in turn, played a song that was sung by their good friend Father Alan at that special 60th birthday party for their dad. It was Elton John's Can you feel the love tonight. I was so grateful for Jon Dyer calling, it was amazing that he felt strongly enough to call me. I just wish that show had been recorded, that was one of the many high points of Bermondsey radio, if you're from round here, you will know exactly what I mean.

Bermondseys number one Dj in Brisbane Australia for the first test.

Page 167 Jimmy Deller Darren Chandler David Cook and Bermondseys number one DJ getting rotten in the Ship aground, Dockhead SE1

Noel – Bermondsey's number one DJ

CHAPTER FOURTEEN

ADMINS AND LISTENERS

Let me introduce some of our loyal listeners.......

Fred and Tina Rowley are a lovely couple, who live just off the Walworth Road, and are a great help to Bermondsey radio, they always listen in, donate, and ask for a few tunes along the way. I learned that Fred worked down the Old Kent Road at the place where they made snooker tables, opposite East Lane, quiet near where JW Parker used to be. Fred himself would go out on the road and install full size tables at pop star mansions, owned by Rod Stewart and Tom Jones. You see, only the best people listen to Bermondsey radio.

Julie Bennett, otherwise known as Ju Bennett, lives in Dartford but heralds from Bermondsey originally, she always listens to our broadcast on a Sunday, she often requests a song in the notice board, and she loves BR. We love all our listeners, especially the ones that take part, so keep tuning in Ju, and don't forget to take part. You know it makes sense.

Trudi P Hart is another one of our regular listeners, Trudi now lives out in Cambridgeshire but is from round here originally. Trudi travelled down to London to attend our big social event and raffle and met all the gang. Trudi often requests a song and takes part in the quiz every now and then, she is one of our many treasured listeners, and long may it continue.

Russell X5 otherwise known as Russell McCloud, McCloud, McCloud, McCloud, McCloud has been with Bermondsey radio since the beginning, Russell always donates, and helps BR out. One day he came round my flat with a bag of Manze's pie and mash, when I was on me uppers, it was delicious. Russell is a very good singer/rapper and does a mean version of Welcome home, an old song made famous by Peters and Lee, but now a big hit with Russell and Wendy. They have covered many songs together and changed the lyrics to promote BR, Russell is a very funny man, and it is always great to be in his company. If you can find him!

Keith Tippett otherwise known as The Master, also, has been with BR right from the very beginning. He donates to BR more regularly than anyone else, knowing that his donations go to our appeal to help Bermondsey kids in our Christmas "Toy Drive", his generosity knows no bounds, and his musical choices in the notice board has earned him his name "The Master" Every single song choice he has made has been spot on. Well, when I say "Every" that's not quite correct. The Master once asked me to play "Chirpy, Chirpy, Cheep, Cheep!" We allow everyone, one mistake, if he does it again, he will be known as Keith.

I am joking of course. Keith has picked some fantastic songs on BR and long may it continue, thanks Keith for all your support.

From the heart of Camberwell, Jaq Hull has been very generous to BR, and she is one of our listeners that take part in everything we do, first to request on the notice board, and if we do seconds, she is always first to respond. Even the Quiz at noon, she gives it a go. I wish all our listeners were like Jaq, she is what Bermondsey radio is all about.

Over the next few chapters some of our admin will write a paragraph or two on BR, and what it meant to them, first up is Wendy Fitzgerald, one of our main sponsors and one of the famous five to tune in on March 20th, 2020.

Hiya my name is *Wendy Fitzgerald*, and I am one of Noel's secret lovers, sorry I mean admins!

I can't even remember how long I have known Noel it's been a long time.... I have been to many parties and pubs where he was DJ. I remember going to the Old Justice one Friday night and he was DJ, I was a bit pissed to say the least and was driving him mad asking for songs in the end he was like ok Wendy! I drove him mad and no doubt to this very day I still do!!....

Like Noel has said I was one of the first people to join Bermondsey Radio and I was the person who encouraged Noel to get a Mic well it was a good idea at the time!...

I have a lot of friends on Facebook but since joining Bermondsey Radio I have made a lot more, some people I have deleted but most I have kept. When I was working, me Kerry & Katy would listen to Noel every day in the office, we would all do the quiz and always request songs. We used to sing along to the songs I can tell you we were like the 3 degrees some would say minus degrees more like! Noel used to entertain us a lot we had so many laughs and so much banter as well as me texting Noel on a regular basis saying stop fucking talking and play the music so hence why I sometimes regretted advising him to get a mic, but later in some shows when he was pissed, and you used to hear him fart or burp or sneeze it cracked me up.

We all used to put comments on the request board, and we used to chat to each other, that's how I met Emma Bowers, Colette Savage, the likes of Katy Hanson, Kerrie Pooke, Carly Britton, Lynne Damiral,

Yvette Chandler, and Keely Brown I have known these lovely ladies a long time. We all got chatting and that's how the throb mob was born! Over the years we have laughed, cried, shit and been sick in front of each other. we have had trips away, which I will not go into, what happens on tour stays on tour!!... I love these ladies Noel always will do.

I still listen, and always will listen to Bermondsey Radio, I have appeared on there a few times and sang with my idol's benny Hill and Russell McCloud, McCloud, McCloud, McCloud, McCloud! we formed "2 bob" and are hoping to appear on Britain's not got talent soon, so watch this space.

Finally, Noel you have helped so many people through this pandemic my god we have sang, danced, cried, and laughed with you. You have been there for us always you say we have helped you, but I don't really think you know how much you have helped all of us.

Keep doing what you are doing Noel as long as you keep playing, we will keep listening. *Wendy Fitzgerald.*

Carly Britton wrote……. I'm Carly Britton and I'm Noels favourite admin really…. Favourite and cheekiest Admin. I remember when Noel first started, and Wendy told me to listen… Noel didn't have a microphone at the time and only a few listeners, but things were about to change for the best. Noel got himself a microphone, 4000 followers and off he went. Noel really brought the community together with the show and his socials and its then that I become part of the Throb Mob along with 8 others. What a cracking bunch of Ladies they are. My highlight on Bermondsey Radio is becoming supreme champion on the quiz whilst pacing the hospital floor in labour. I will never forget that moment or the pain. Thanks, Noel, for Bermondsey Radio, the friends,

the socials and bringing everyone together at a tough time. You are a
kind man. Be proud, be very proud.

Sharon Saunders is one of the original listeners on BR and has a heart
of gold. Back in March 2020 she was requesting all sorts of songs, John
Holt, Amy Winehouse, The Real thing, to name but a few. Sadly,
tragedy struck the family when her husband Terry Saunders passed
away on December 14th, 2020. This was an incredibly sad time for
everyone. We made plans to give Terry a fantastic send-off, and on the
6th of January 2021, the day he was laid to rest, BR and Sharon, his wife,
organized a special musical tribute to be broadcast after the funeral.
These were the times when certain restrictions were still in place, so all
the mourners made their way home and listened-in to BR, a very
personal service followed, in Terry's memory. All the songs were
chosen by the family and their wonderful friends. Paige Barritt came on
the phone and made a wonderful speech as did Terry's son Bobby. It
was very emotional, and I do believe Bermondsey radio helped Sharon
and all her family and friends on that day.

Bermondsey radio is a tiny little station in comparison to all the other
massive stations out there. The main advantage that BR has over its
rivals is that we can get away with almost anything we want. We play
what we want, say what we want, and do what we want. It's very easy,
but out listeners love it. It is quiet worrying when people meet me
down the pub and the first thing they say is "I heard you last night,
pissed as a newt on Bermondsey radio!" who, me pissed?? I have been
broadcasting almost three years, and I admit been drunk just three
times on air, how did they manage to tune in on one of these three
occasions?? Makes me laugh. It's a bit like someone taking a first
impression of you. If I walk into a pub and fail to say hello to everyone
in the pub, the one person I miss out, will always believe me to be
ignorant, as I didn't acknowledge them. So therefore, I must always be
aware of it and try and spread myself around. I love to leave the mic on

while I am broadcasting a show, then I will start munching an apple, works a treat. "Noel, your mic is on!" I have had many a laugh doing that little stunt. If I must go to the toilet while on air, I'll try and put a twelve incher on the decks, to give me plenty of time to get to the khazi and back! If I am feeling very mischievous, I will leave the mic on and start cursing as I arrive back to the laptop, it's a cracker, always entertains, Simon Bates couldn't do that! The best bit of radio I do is silence, when my door entry bell goes off, it normally is an Amazon delivery, invariably I am talking on the mic live on air, when it goes off. I must disconnect wires, headphones, and move laptop to one side, jump up off the armchair, turn towards the door and let them in, via the entry phone system. I leave the mic on, sometimes deliberately, and the listener is imagining what the hell is going on here! The beauty of radio is your imagination, while listening, please let your imagination wander, you will enjoy the BR experience so much better. When I return to the laptop, I will swear a few times and say, "Oh shit, I've left the mic on!" that's how we do things on BR, entertaining the listeners, always.

Bermondsey radio has its own free app on Android, you can find it in the play store, on Google, just search Bermondsey radio. It has got great features, like getting reminders on broadcast times and a very good signal reception. Most listeners Bluetooth the audio to a smart speaker or direct to their smart tv. There are many ways to tune in to BR, the most popular way is using your tv, it must have a internet connection, and use the tv's browser to type "radioing" into its search engine, the sound will be wonderful. A bit of advice, the signal you receive will be great if no other device is draining your usage, for example someone is streaming on a laptop in another room. This can weaken the strength of signal from BR, and you may have to retune to get it back.

My name is *Colette Savage,* and I am really Noel's favorite admin. I was introduced to Bermondsey radio by the infamous Jackie O'Brien and my little sister Louise. I'm so glad I joined the group; the music and the laughs kept me going through the lockdown. Being so far away from friends and family up here in the northeast of Scotland seemed much further during covid. Noel did a fantastic job of bringing the community together and without the station I wouldn't have met the rest of the throb mob, who are the best kind of people. I'll be forever thankful to Bermondsey radio for that. *Colette Savage.*

My name is Keely Brown, and I am Noel's favorite Admin.

March 2020 will stay with us forever. The world changed and no one knew what was to come. At first, we heard of Coronavirus which had affected some people in China. None of us really took much notice it was just news from a faraway place and then things started to get serious.

I had met Noel several times doing his gigs in pubs and one or two parties over the years. His musical taste is very similar to mine, and he had always got people up dancing.

We had been Facebook friends for a while although we didn't really have much contact. I was curious to see he was planning a broadcast at the beginning of lockdown. So, I tuned in. I think at the time he had between five and ten listeners. I remember this so clearly; I was cleaning my bathroom and I requested a song. It was Somebody Help Me Out by Beggar and Co and within five minutes I got a mention and my song played. Happy days, so my friendship with Bermondsey radio began.

I started to listen in every day, request a song and join in with the midday quiz. I am going to brag about the quiz a little – forgive me. So,

I won several times in a row, my main "rival" was Darren Chandler who has a bloody good knowledge of music. One particular day there was a steward's enquiry into the spelling of Jamiroquai. It went on for days, but it was all good fun with no hard feelings. Several listeners were crowned "supreme champion" for winning multiple days in a row and on BR's first anniversary, Noel put on a quiz just for all the supreme champions. I only went and won it!! My prize was to present a show with Noel which was absolutely brilliant to do. I still remain BR's only ever "supreme, supreme champion" A very proud moment!

As more and more listeners joined us, Noel was struggling to run things smoothly. He was juggling many plates with jingles, adverts, requests, the quiz, birthday shout outs etc. So, he asked for some help and his Admin team was born. We are all there to help him and keep him in check. If you have ever heard a "tipsy" Noel on the radio, you will know what I mean.

A few of the admin ladies had a WhatsApp group. There was Wendy (who I knew very well) Yvette (who I also knew) Kerrie (who I knew when she was a little girl) then Emma, Carly, Lynne, Colette, and Katy none of whom I had met. We were going to be called The Real Housewives of Bermondsey (TRHOB) but written down it looks like Throb and so we became known as The Throb Mob. As the eldest member of the group, I soon earned the nickname The Throb Mother and I can honestly say these girls are the absolute best. We have all formed an unbreakable bond and soon to embark on our second Throbbers on tour trip. I love them all.

One of my hobbies is poetry. Not the Keats/Wordsworth type but more like silly ditties and odes. I wrote a poem one day about Bermondsey radio and Noel decided he liked it and created "poetry corner" every Friday at 1pm. Each week I would get my thinking cap on and knock up a little rhyme. I also wrote some for birthdays and special occasions.

As lockdown eased off and over time life went back to "normal" Noel's shows reduced as people started to go out again. To this day he continues with his super Sunday shows and still has a fair few listeners. Oh, and the quiz still exists. And yes, I do still win on the odd occasion.

What can I say about Noel – he is just a nice man. Everything he did (and still does) for Bermondsey Radio, is out of kindness. He succeeded in keeping people's spirits up in an extremely worrying and unprecedented time in history. He never got paid for any of it. Just requesting some donations so he could keep going. So, from me – Thank you Noel. I don't think you will ever know how many people you helped and how many friendships you created.

Bermondsey radio has taught me several things. People are kind and good and nice. I still love poetry. Keep your friends close. Soul music is timeless. And I think my bathroom is due another clean. KJB 2022

Clare Pascoe wrote ……My name is Clare Pascoe and I'm Noel's favorite admin. Bermondsey radio was a god send during lockdown! I heard about it in May 2020 by Debbie Holley, and I've not looked back since. When I started listening there was no talking just pure music gold from the brilliant Noel Smyth whom I remembered from my 'Lil' days. Without fail at 10.30am every day I would tune in and request a song, songs were played that I haven't heard for years, mainly the 80's era and lots of soul, which was my favorite, and it was the best, and I would take part in the quiz at noon. I was addicted to Bermondsey Radio and Noel Smyth's dulcet tones and still am today. Sadly, when I had to return to work, I couldn't listen in live so thankfully Noel would repeat it later in the day and I would listen on my way home from work in the car. To top it all off, I was asked to become an admin, which I was overjoyed and still am proud to be part of this littlest, biggest radio station- Thanks Noel for everything xx *Clare Pascoe.*

My name is *Julie Ann Gifford,* and I am Noel's favorite admin, Can I just thank Noel & BR for making me feel very welcome not coming from Bermondsey I was welcomed with open arms Noel you certainly kept me and many others sane during the covid pandemic it was such a tough time for us all, but you kept us all entertained throughout thank you from the bottom of my heart. I will always have a piece of BR here every time I see my lovely awning thank you x Julie *Ann Gifford.*

Lee Ellis wrote.......

Living away from my roots has been difficult at times especially during Covid and working from home, when BR started broadcasting during the week it made a shitty time become bearable and I felt in touch with my former life. Old friends and new also helped get though our shittiest days, the burping, farting, delivery men, gas man we heard it all, the peeing and the odd fucking and blinding made it real, and a bit of normality was given back to us. Every time I hear 'simply the Best' 'you don't bring me flowers' 'you're beautiful' a smile appears, and BR is on the forefront on my mind. You always thank us the listeners, but the hard work, loyalty and dedication is all thanks to you Mr. Smyth. You and BR honestly got me through such horrible times and that I will be eternally grateful. If and when I win the lottery .... LOL you are one of the people I would love to help.... Nice little home in Goa with your own nightclub maybe???? Thanks for the music and being you Xx   *Lee Ellis.*

Dave London (Tenerife) Wrote There we were up in the hills of Los Cristianos in the first few days of lockdown wondering how long it was going to last and what were we going to do all day unable to venture out apart from the permitted walk to the shop for essential provisions. Then Jean spots a post about Noel trying to set up a radio station and the first test broadcast to be the next Sunday. We both thought we'll give it a try and history were made. At first it was just music requested by text no links or ads, but you could basically ask for any tune and "The Man" found it and sent it over the airwaves. Gradually radio application used was updated and sound quality improved until we are where we are today. But in those first few weeks Bermondsey Radio was a link back to the world we had left behind and broke the feeling of isolation being in a new country unable to meet up with anyone else to talk to. Cheers Noel that's why you are Bermondsey's No1! *Dave London (Tenerife).*

Lynne Damiral wrote

Well Bermondsey radio and Covid, interesting combination, but it worked. The listeners gradually increased, we all felt part of a community, still do. I know a good few people on BR, who are friends, or friends of friends. It was like going in a room hearing music and news. Even while driving in a car. I was watching the live draw on the M5. We had good news, out of Bermondsey radio, The food bank, to help people, the Toy Drive, we had babies born, weddings, birthdays, and some sad news. The What's app group pinging, when we heard something, we shouldn't of. Laughing, like toilet breaks and burps. In the early days we laughed so much about the new microphone and noel forgetting to turn it off. It brought people together from all over the country and different countries. during difficult times. What a great achievement to come out of covid. I have made new friends for life. It kept me going at work. which was a lonely place during covid. It's not capital radio. it's better. Let's not forget the laughs of Benny Hill ...he came with us to our holiday. I have a photo to prove...yes Benny Hill was in the house .and our own in-house poet and the same time. Virtual parties. And finally live on Facebook raffle draws. And not forgetting the throb mob you know who you are. Thanks for the music, Noel long may it continue *Lynne Damiral*

Birthday shout outs happen every Sunday at 1pm during the Super Sunday show and are very important to our listeners, let me explain why. Firstly, this radio station is a family, so we look after the people that look after us. In the Facebook group we publish virtual Birthday cards, and our members gladly wish our fellow members a happy birthday. Secondly Its polite, and finally its good manners. I have lost count of the times I have presented a virtual birthday party for our listeners or Admin. The person celebrating their birthday will compile a playlist and throughout the virtual party my job is to play the songs in some sort of order. We have had some classic virtual parties, and the good thing about it is, many people tune in. Great songs are played, and the guests are all over the country dancing round the coffee table, or out in the garden munching on a barbecued lamb chop while tapping their toes to George Benson. Remember, virtual parties are because we were not allowed to mix and had to stay apart from each other. They helped Bermondsey radio survive. The fun, the music, the donations, it's all because of the virtual birthday parties, that helped keep BR on the air.

Sometimes I sit and wonder, how did I get into this position? I have not written anything since I left school, so how can I be writing my own autobiography? I might have written the odd email, here and there, but thousands of words have been written for the book so far! Is there no stopping me? What started me off? Why did I begin? I really don't know the answers, but now that I have started, I am determined to make it an enjoyable read. I think it's a way of being able to thank the people that helped me through the Covid19 nightmare. Yes, I know I helped you, but my God, you all helped me.

In my life, I always react to negatives in a positive way, so if someone puts me down, I bounce up even stronger. They will never win because I have an inner determination that won't allow me to lose. Even though I have suffered from depression for many years I always battle back. I know my haters very well, just look at my "friends" on Facebook, who never "Like" my posts! These same people never helped me when I was broke and practically begging for donations to keep BR on air. Their ignorance and lack of generosity spurred me on, you see, their negativity turned into my positivity. I am the one with my own radio station, I am the one who is the author of this book. I helped hundreds of my local community through Covid, and I will keep on going, as long as they keep listening.

There is nowhere more patriotic than Bermondsey, when I moved here in 1969 it was very clear. Every time the national anthem was sung, it was with pride, and a stout heart. As I am writing this book Her Majesty Queen Elizabeth II has died, the world, the country, London and here in Bermondsey, we are all in a state of shock. I am grateful, and thankful I have lived during her reign. I loved her like my own grandmother, with respect and admiration. I am tearful, emotional, and very proud of our Queen at this sad time, my instinct is to play music in honor of her life this coming weekend, the 11th of September 2022. You see, this is what BR is all about, this is what we do, this is what Bermondsey people do. God save the King.

Hundreds tuned in to our special show, great music was played, mostly chosen by our listeners. While playing these emotionally charged songs, I watched, on tv, her Majesties coffin travelling through the Scottish countryside and the silent respect of the Scottish people as she travelled through the towns and cities. Thank you, Scotland, that was pure class.

The hundreds of thousands that walked from Southwark Park to Westminster Hall was fantastic, and hats off to David Beckham, who walked the walk, while others just talked the talk.

Finally, we came to Monday 19th September when Her Majesty Queen Elizabeth II was laid to rest. What a fantastic farewell. I had a drink for Her Majesty, down The Ship aground, then took a stroll down the Bank public house, which was packed, and now run by Jimmy Shilling, who is doing a very good job down there, Jimmy also is in business with Simon Steers with Millreef signs, who are a major sponsor of Bermondsey radio. I left the Bank worse for wear, I staggered home, good job I had the next day off work. I never moved all day, dying on the sofa. Long live the King.

Bermondsey radio, over the past two years have broadcast many patriotic shows, V.E Day, Colonel Tom's funeral, The Duke of Edinburgh's funeral, the Queen's Platinum jubilee, all remembrance Sunday's and now Her Majesty Queen Elizabeth II funeral, we broadcast three musical tributes. I am very proud to have played music at these memorable events, they meant a lot to me and my listeners. Always well received and so many more listeners tuned in.

Sadly, another great friend of BR 's passed away, after a short illness, Pat Sharp died last year on the 4th of July 2022. She was the loveliest of ladies. I remember her at my school St Michaels, a few years older than me and she had a wonderful smile and great personality. She married the club captain of Fisher, Dennis Sharp, best captain they have ever had, even to this day, and a fine gentleman. They would tune in to BR and have me play Frank Sinatra and a great Carole Bayer Sager & Peter Allan penned song called You and me (we wanted it all). They both had great taste in music and Dennis often texts me for their special song. I decided to dedicate a special show for Pat, and it was a very emotionally charged show, with hundreds tuning in and participating with dedications for Pat and sincere condolences to her husband Dennis and all the family. I attended the funeral service at Dockhead Church, on what would have been Pat and Dennis's 50th Wedding Anniversary. I saw many faces from the past, old-school mates, drinking pals. But my main reason for being there was to pay my respects to a lovely lady and shake hands with Dennis and other members of the family. It was a great service, with great words from Dennis, and so many people there. Pat Sharp you were loved by so many, and your family did you proud.

Noel – Bermondsey's number one DJ

Emma Bowers (Noel's favourite Admin) writes… What does Bermondsey Radio means to me, Emma Bowers or as I'm better known "Noel's favourite Admin? In a word "Everything". 2020 was probably the worst year of my life, for a lot of reasons. It started with the breakup of a 9-year relationship. Then the news that my best friend had the worst form of breast cancer there is and subsequently a long and hard fight on her hands. Then my own health issue, one I would need surgery for. And with all this then came Covid. I was made to WFH like the rest of the country and ike many people, I felt isolated and alone, but I was given a tiny light in the darkness. I was told about a fella who was a regular DJ in all the local Bermondsey boozers, that had started a radio station online and was really good. You could join his FB group "Bermondsey Radio" and request a song along with a shout out, or message for your loved ones. I joined straight away and was addicted in minutes. The DJ Noel or as I came to call him "Boss Man", did an excellent job but wanted more for his listeners and ever-growing loyal members. As time went on the show evolved, a microphone was introduced and we suddenly had Noel's dulcet tones blaring through our speakers, along with all our favourite songs. Then came the quiz, birthday shout outs and even a "Poetry Corner". Every day I'd wait patiently for the show to start and would be saddened at the ending, for those few hours online, it was like I was in a room filled with lots of love, laughter, and friends. In fact, I made some real friends. 8 in fact, of amazing women and through this friendship the "Throb Mob" was formed. Noel brought together 9 women, some who had met or knew each other in one way, but some that had never met before. We are now 9 of the closest companions and to this day we are grateful to

Noel and BR for introducing us through music, laughter, and good old Bermondsey banter. In fact, I'm writing this from my bed after the second TMOT2022…. It was hardcore as you can probably imagine, but I'll leave the details to your imagination. Thank you, Noel, for being the community's saviour through the pandemic and mine, through the worst time in my life. From the bottom of my heart, you are, and will forever be, my "Boss Man" *Emma Bowers.*

Yvette Chandler wrote………

what does "Bermondsey radio " mean to me, I am Yvette Chandler one of Noel's admins. It lifted my spirits when these were desperate times and everyday listening was like one big party. What Bermondsey Radio did was gave us hope that we would all be back together one day. Music is the one thing that brings people together and everyone enjoys but it wasn't just the music, it was so much more, everyday there was the quiz and our own resident poet Keely, Noel would play Wendy's famous rendition of "Ernie" , raising money for local charity's, there was something for everyone going on every day and for those few hours of normality it helped us all to forget what nightmare was going on outside our doorsteps. To think that was all started by one person out of the goodness of his heart. He brought back those good times of great music, in some of the best pubs, what more could you ask for? Living in Kent away from my family and friends was hard but having that link for those few hours a day it made you laugh, cry (typical me) and gave you something else to focus on. What Bermondsey Radio has done is brought together a community of families, along with new and old friends and still does to this day but I must thank Noel for not only the best music but for a great bunch of lifelong friends that all started from Bermondsey radio "The Throb Mob" Thank you Noel

Claire Rayner writes...... We received an invitation on Facebook to join Bermondsey Radio March 2020 and lockdown was introduced. Noel got us through the days playing live shows 7 days a week with additional shows Thursday – Sunday evenings playing fantastic music. I become one of the admins for the Facebook page when Noel put out a request for help, we have had some great laughs in the group chat getting Noel in a Mucking Fuddle whilst live on air. The quiz caused some controversary on several occasions, it was only a bit of fun!!!!

My lovely dad was diagnosed with cancer of the oesophagus March 2020. Noel would give him a shout out, send him good wishes over the air waves my dad loved it (made him feel important lol). Noel really helped lift his spirits, I am truly grateful for that. During one of Dad's hospital admissions, he called me saying "the same f***king 4 songs have been playing over & over is there a problem?" I laughed and told him "You've been listening to the loop songs Noel plays when off air" his response "your F**king joking aint ya I've been listening for about an hour or two" We had a good laugh. Happy to say my dad's operation was a success.

Christmas 2020 was approaching Sarah King organised a collection between all admin to get a gift for Noel so he could have a good Christmas, our way of letting him know we care. We put together a hamper of various food items, bottle of gold watch (whisky) one in a million-pint glass, Bermondsey Radio t-shirt & cap and other bits and pieces also a Christmas card with £100 inside. A week or so before Christmas I, Sarah, Julie, Beckie, Emma all rocked up to Noel's flat to surprise him and deliver the hamper. He couldn't work out how we go in his block but us women are very persuasive, he was very shocked, speechless, and overwhelmed by it all.

We continue to tune in on Sunday's and support Noel. We would like to say thank you Noel for creating a fantastic radio station, arranging the socials so we could all meet and being the kind caring person that you are. I don't think you know how much some of us appreciate you, Lots of love *Claire & Dazo Millwall Markham.*

My Set-up for Wedding in Tunbridge Wells during the lockdown, only 50 guests were allowed

CHAPTER FIFTEEN

BIG HEARTS

When I started BR, I never imagined it would still be going strong thirty months later. The luck we had was incredible. The technical aspect was a miracle on its very own. The times I would sit at my laptop and fiddle with various protocols and configurations to get us broadcasting was numerous. Somehow it all fell into place in March 2020. The next thing you need is help, one person cannot do this on their own. My admin has been fantastic throughout, in every way, very supportive, innovative, and most of all, they care. They care about Bermondsey radio and help me in so many ways.

The sponsors put their money where their mouth is and have radio adverts broadcasting all around the world every Sunday, and 24/7 on my sound cloud account. The listeners, without them, I would be talking to myself, which I often find myself doing these days while waiting for a C10 on Jamaica road on my way to work. We had lots of support from regular donators, but in our team, we had Ian Rooney, a person who helped Bermondsey radio like a man determined to get us through to the end. He was Bermondsey radio's "Roy Keane" and we will forever be grateful to his tenacity, generosity and his leadership, and without Ian Rooney we would never have made it through. Sharon Rooney, his wife was also a fantastic help, and was our first sponsor with her business "Nellies Flowers".

Sharon helped with donating bunches of flowers for our raffles and loads of other stuff. It was Ian and Sharon's idea to organise a raffle and their idea paid off. I was overanxious due to my depression, my hopes of getting profit through the raffle was not optimistic, But Ian soon settled my worrying and anxiety by knocking out loads of raffle tickets at the Glebe sports ground clubhouse after a home game for his beloved Stansfeld FC. I mentioned on air one evening that I fancied a "Gold watch" (Scotch) and minutes later I had an Uber delivery courtesy of the Rooney's, a bottle of Jameson whiskey and a large bottle of coke! A couple of hours later I was rotten as a pear, slurring all my introductions, and effing and blinding as I went along. This, of course was hilarious to the listeners, imagine Simon Bates saying, "I fucking love Barry White!". Or something to that effect.

Nicki Whiting, one of our greatest supporters of Bermondsey radio, sent me an Uber delivery too, a bottle of whiskey! anyone would think I am an alcoholic! It was very kind of Nicki, and I had a few drams that night. In two years of shows I only drank on a few occasions, but you see people remember the shows with me a bit drunk, makes me laugh, it really does. Some of the shows at night we would have a great laugh. I really hope my listeners don't think I go round drunk, burping, farting, and swearing like a trooper. It is all done for comedic value, although the whiskey does help my "act". My shows always contain something fun that my listeners can latch on to. I would go to bed at night and lie there, thinking of ways of how I could make my listeners laugh, make them feel special. In years to come will people realise how lonely and isolated we all felt? Bermondsey radio went a long way in helping that feeling of solitude. Turn the station on, and hey presto, you were in the company of like-minded people. Music lovers yearning for company through the Facebook group page, requesting songs and hearing their names on the radio. The thrill of having your name pronounced over the airwaves is a great feeling and is addictive. Is it any wonder, we had a captive audience while Covid had a grip of our nation. Now, things are much more relaxed, and the pandemic is in the background, yet, on Sunday's Bermondsey radio has at least five hundred listeners that tune in.

Generosity is a word I have used a lot in this book, one of our main sponsors is Newold scaffolding and Martin Fitzgerald. He and Wendy, his wife, have helped Bermondsey radio beyond belief. They have a fantastic advert I made for them, featuring Yazz & the plastic population singing the only way is up! Due to the fact they are always erecting scaffolding around town. Wendy delivered Christmas dinner for me on Christmas day last year after the morning radio show, and it was very nice indeed. That was very kind of her, and these kind gestures is what Bermondsey radio is all about.

When you are writing a book it's important to include and mention those people that went the extra mile, there was so many people like this, that bent over backwards to help keep Bermondsey radio on air. The difficult bit is NOT repeating yourself, but as I have stated before, I have never written anything like this before so please excuse me if I mention you twice and an even bigger apology if I don't remember you at all. I can assure you I am not doing it on purpose, and I will endeavour to make this book as complete as I possibly can. For example, I have Keely and Colette helping me with the finishing of the book, making sure all the punctuation marks, spelling, and grammar are looking good.

Steve and Georgie Chandler are a wonderful couple that listen to Bermondsey radio when they can. They have donated throughout and to our "Toy drive" which is dear to their hearts. Steve in the early days would like to take part in the quiz and did very well at it. Steve also came up with the idea to include a prize of three songs to the winner of the quiz, which the winner would get played before the quiz the next day. They would also get a virtual trophy in the Facebook group page.

Questions would be set in the Facebook group page by Carly or Darren on various subjects like "who did the best version of you make me feel brand new" by the Stylistics or Simply red? And "what was your favourite boozer down the Old Kent Road?" These questions would conjure up some fantastic response by members that you would not normally see taking part, so this was a revelation to see these dormant members suddenly getting involved. I mean these great questions posed by my fabulous admins would get over 200 replies each. I wish they would take part more often, keep the station buzzing.

I must thank Nina and Alan Lewington my good friends from the boatman pub and now living in Bexleyheath, they have always helped Bermondsey radio with donations right from the very beginning and still to this day help in whatever way they can. I know they love requesting songs and listening to the shows, they have been brilliant to Bermondsey radio in every way.

Joanne McAlea and her husband Trevor have been tuning in and donating since the beginning, loving the tunes, and dancing round the kitchen, having shout outs to their friends, and enjoying the personability of BR. Joanne and Trevor are a lovely couple, lifelong sweethearts, that met in the Fellmongers, Trevor loves old soul dance tunes, one of his favourites is Dynasty "I just begun to love you" I play it when I can for them, they are treasured BR listeners.

Most weddings I have performed at have all gone smoothly and without a hitch. This wedding I am about to tell you about was the Wedding from hell. Not because of the lovely couple who got married, because they were wonderful people. It was the logistics of the wedding itself that went wonky. It all ended up well in the end, I am pleased to say, but for a while there it all started to fall apart at the seams, let me explain…

I set off extra early, this was going to be a long day, it was eleven o'clock in the morning and the journey out to Bromley was set into the sat-nav for directions, where would we be without sat-navs? I passed Magpie hill golf club, and I was being directed down a dirt track opposite the nine-hole golf course. There was a large house at the bottom of the track and when I arrived not a soul was around, looked like a Gypsy site, with a caravan at one side and load of old metal at the other. I knocked on the door, nothing, not a whisper. I got back into the van There was a nudge on my passenger side window. It was a black and white Friesian cow steaming up the window with each breath, while it was chewing the cud. Starring at me. The cow shit the life out of me. Where had this lonesome cow come from? Where were his mates? I turned the van around and headed back to the main road. I wasn't panicking just yet, but I drove for the next hour with no joy whatsoever. I was now in a field, cow pats everywhere, the tyres were covered in yellow cow shit, not a good look. I thought I better have a steward's enquiry into the venue instructions given to me by the wedding organiser. There was a road in Beckenham with the same name, with a very similar post code, it was my last chance I was going to head for there. You see, nobody was picking up their phones to help me, they were all in the bloody church with their phones switched off!

It was the right choice to make this was the correct address and I pulled up in front of their drive looking like my van had just finished the rally-cross championship of Great Britain. Grass, daisies, and mud were all stuck all over the lower section of my van. I was greeted at the front door by a young boy around twelve years of age and he showed me through to the marquee. My heart sunk. The house was a long posh one, with an even bigger garden. I knew I had to get the sound and light through the house, onto the patio, walk the whole length of the garden and then set it up at the end of the marquee! I was sweating buckets.

Two hours later I had trudged the equipment through the obstacles of this assault course of a wedding reception and given it a good old sound and light test. The guests were arriving and my deejaying hadn't even started yet, all I could think of is, I have ten more hours of this, and somehow must get all this equipment back into my van, and long after midnight. As it turned out I was determined to make it a special day for the newlyweds and played my little heart out for them. After I had said my goodbyes and loaded everything into the van, I sat in the driver's seat exhausted, but satisfied, I had done my best, they were all happy with my work, I would sleep well tonight.

People ask me "What now for Bermondsey's number one DJ?" firstly, I want to get even better. Always improving. The sound, the light, my performance there is always room for improvement. I personally believe I am better now at controlling a party than I have ever been. I would love to be the stadium announcer at the Den and introduce new ways of getting the fans round up and giving the players an extra edge on the pitch. I have the experience and confidence to do it, maybe one day it might happen. I would love to play musical snippets at a one-day cricket match for Kent or Surrey, but not the usual songs, something completely different, a new approach that will galvanise the home team into victory. I would like to play in a pub residency preferably in the Bermondsey area at the weekends to entertain the locals with songs from their youth and bring back the memories of days gone by. Raise money for our "Toy drive" to help make a fantastic Christmas for our local kids, we will continue to do this, and hope you can help me in this very worthwhile cause. I would like Bermondsey radio to continue on a Sunday morning and help our community through this financial crisis. Realistically, taking into account my age, opportunity is not going to be easy, but if anything does come along, I will gladly grab hold of it with both hands and do it to the best of my ability. Anyone wants to give it a whirl, let me know.

Another great venue I played was down at the Spa Hotel in Royal Tunbridge Wells, it was a 40th wedding anniversary and packed with local people. This venue was quality, and the staff were very helpful indeed. Its nice to play top venues around the country. I don't mind traveling thirty miles from home, but anything more and it becomes a bit of a chore. A place I enjoy playing is down at Eastchurch on the Isle of Sheppey, its run by Aaron Mace, and a very nice fella, he always has top entertainment there at the Palm Tree Sports bar and the food is out of this world. I did the recent platinum jubilee celebrations for Her

Majesty the Queen down at the club. It was well attended and so many faces from Bermondsey, it was like playing down Jamaica road.

Just recently I have been playing regularly down at the St Johns centre in Larcom street just off the Walworth Road. Deleney Brown is the lady in charge down there and has now booked me for the second New Year's party in a row. The Walworth roaders are very friendly people, and it is a very easy venue to get to. The last time I was there in September, for an eighty's music night, it was a great party with lots of dancing and drinking, love my Walworth friends. I have been playing music for forty-three years and Deleney made me a list of 125 songs!! I normally ask for a list of 15-20 to give me an idea of the music they would like played. 125 songs is a unique list, but it made sure we had a blinding night.

The smallest pub I have ever worked is down Chislehurst near the station, its called Ramblers rest, I did the opening of the pub when It was refitted, very nice and sleek looking but very claustrophobic inside, very nice beer garden, and I remember they had lovely barmaids. I worked there one New Year's Eve and it all ended in tears, as the guvnor insisted, I let a string vest sing on my mic, you all know how much I hate pub singers, especially when they try and sing on my mic. That was the final straw, I packed up and was out of there, and never returned to that Tom Thumb of a pub again.

Back in the day I would play the old Scout house down Jamaica road near the Boatman's, for the Boatman's football team. This was a great venue for a good old knee up, and I would have to say, some of my best work was done here for my good friends. Big Al, Bonzo, Teddy Gorman and all the ladies. I recall Charlie Nunn (Black cab driver) said to me "Noel, that was a fantastic night". It was always nice to be complemented on my efforts, it made me happy. They later moved their venue to behind Stamford Street it didn't quite work, not the same acoustics, wasn't as good as the scout hall. The Boatman lads would call me "Bonecrusher" due to my placid peaceful demeanour, in contrast to the American heavyweight boxer, who had a killer instinct. Oh, the irony.

Always have fancied playing music at the London Marathon on Jamaica road, nobody has ever asked me, but I would love to play all those great songs as all the runners jogged by. I live on the other side of the road to the Gregorian pub I would do it if someone provided the electricity and a tent to keep dry (If it rained) and I would provide the sound system. I am just thinking of all those uplifting songs that I could play. Maybe one day someone will ask me.

Whenever I play music in the suburbs of South-east London, I always attract a large crowd of Bermondsey ex pats, somehow, they find out that I will be there, and they come out in their droves. The best case of this was In Eltham and Sidcup and the Beehive and Charcoal Burner respectfully. On the May bank holiday Sunday Stan Smith, the owner of the Charcoal Burner told me that he took £10,000 on that Sunday afternoon, and he didn't take that the whole week. I will say it till I am blue in the face, pub singers are so bad its embarrassing, they dress the part, but sound so pitchy. In a half empty pub, they sound fine, with their radio mics and cultured speakers. But the idea is to pack the pub out with ladies dancing their socks off and getting the men to drink themselves silly. This is not going to happen with a glorified Frank Sinatra, or Adele lookalike. Unless you find a singer that has a range of all musical genres and has a range of 10,000 songs, like I have.

I was so good for the Charcoal Burner that the Beehive booked me for every Saturday night for almost three years! And every Saturday night that I worked there it was packed solid, they took a fortune, every Saturday night for 150 weeks. Now just think about it, I have a radio station that can promote your bar to its listeners and then they will talk about it and turn up for a fantastic gathering of people that love dance music, at the time that you want them there. It's a no brainer, if it worked before, it would work with radio promotion and the success of this book or am I dreaming? They might not like Lou Rawls anymore, or Teddy and Luther. They might think I am too old and should hang up my headphones. The target audience is over forties who like to go out at the weekend and let their hair down, they dress up and they want to party, they love the music that I play, and the way I play it. I think this might work, what do you think?

On the other hand, you could book Patrick, one of the nicest guys you're ever likely to meet, he is better than any pub singer I have heard. Come on what you want to dance to? A pitchy Frank Sinatra? Or a Toni Braxton dance mix? He has the record collection, the patter on the mic and he presents himself well. I don't know how I got the tag "Bermondsey's number one" but surely Patrick is the best at what he does, you are guaranteed a great party with him playing the tunes. Great sound system and lighting he has got the lot. I have heard some mickey mouse deejays who play in the Bermondsey area, but Patrick is the number one DJ as far as I am concerned. More importantly, he is a very generous guy, I have lost count the number of times he has given me bookings over the years, if I ever get round to having my sixtieth birthday party, there is only one man for the job, that is the brilliant Patrick.

The point I am making is, by all means book a pitchy pub singer, and maybe let them do two forty-five-minute sets, but if you want a proper knees up, you have to finish the night with a DJ like Patrick.

I have worked with some fantastic singers in my DJ career, I spent five years on a cruise ship with some excellent baritones, one guy who stands out was from Manchester and would often sing at Main Road, Manchester city's social club, when he wasn't working on the liners. His name was Frank Ford and boy could he sing. He taught the great impressionist Mike Yarwood how to impersonate Sinatra, Dean Martin, Matt Monro, he was a fantastic guy with a great fun personality, when he did his version of Bing Crosby on stage in the ship's theatre hairs on the back of my neck would stand up. He was never a pub singer, too bloody good. He would regularly get standing ovations for his rendition of "Music of the night" from Phantom of the opera. The worst singer I worked with at the Bermondsey carnival was Alexander O'Neal, he was still a showman, but his voice was flat, it had lost its range. Gwen Dickey from Rose Royce had the best vocal range from all the stars I worked with at the carnival, she was very nervous going on stage, but once she was there, she glided through "Wishing on a star" and "Love don't live here anymore" with a lot of class and made it look easy.

I must admit, quite honestly, i am coming to the end of my reign as Bermondsey's number one DJ. I think it is about time to hang up my headphones. I am no spring chicken anymore! I am referring to my mobile work, it's the physicality of it. Setting up my sound and light system is hard work these days. Unloading the van into the venue and setting up is stressful to say the least. Once it is set up and I start playing the music I am in my element, and I love every second of it. I love making people dance. But, when the night comes to an end, it is more difficult to get everything back into the van. Just picking audio cables up, is a major task these days, and getting four 25kg active speakers back into the van takes some doing. However, how do I say goodbye? Music always comes first, I have a booking in February, that might be my last one, unless someone else books me. Who knows I could still be playing music at parties for years to come, oh the indecision.

Bermondsey radio, now that is altogether different. But it's not cheap. If I have a job and funds to do so, we can carry on if we have listeners. The good news is that there is no physicality involved in broadcasting the station. I sit in my armchair with my laptop on my lap, with a lapel mic attached to my t-shirt, and away we go. Its looking good for Bermondsey radio as long as I have a job.

I went on a Caribbean cruise to see what it was like to be a passenger, rather than being a member of the entertainment staff. The cruise ship I worked on was just 12,500 tonnes, this ship was 67,000 tones, quite a lot bigger. I flew out to Barbados and the coaches met us on the tarmac and straight to the ship. My case was waiting for me at my cabin door. The cabin door key was a credit card shape and held all details for purchasing drinks and items from the retail outlets dotted around the ship. I went on an excursion to visit the island of Mustique, just south of St Vincent and the Grenadines. Mick Jagger has a home here and Princess Margaret spent many winters on this Caribbean sunshine Island. We travelled on a catamaran in the glorious November sunshine and were escorted by flying fish and a handful of dolphins. One of the crew caught a four-foot swordfish on our way out to the island. We had lunch paid for included in the excursion price and we all sat down at a restaurant on the beach, it was lovely. After the meal had a relaxing couple of hours by the sea, was offered some Marijuana by the looky looky man and a massage by a local lady, it was all happening. We all boarded the catamaran and after a few pictures the captain set us on course back to our ship in the port of St Vincent. Halfway back the vessel broke down. The engine just stopped. We were drifting in the middle of the Caribbean Sea and the captain looked worried. One of the lady passengers had a pair of stockings in her handbag, she handed it to one of the crew and with her permission they used them for a temporary fan belt, and it worked. I wasn't sure why she was carrying tights in her handbag on such a trip, but she got the vessel up and running again. Well done to that lady. By the time we got back to the ship it was just getting dark and the captain onboard was blowing his horn full blast. We were late and holding the ship up, we all started to trot to the applause of the passengers above us looking over the ship's railings. All aboard, the ship was off to its next port and the beautiful island of Granada.

I went on a party cruise with a steel band playing reggae classics with a bit of calypso thrown in. They had a great band and singer on board, and everyone took part in a spot of limbo on the top deck of the boat. I got as low as five feet, and was eliminated early on, eventually a slim elastic young lady won the bottle of rum with a height of about three feet. She was bendy.

Another holiday in Marbella, I don't really like it very much, too many posers with no real money at all, yet they stroll around in Gucci flip flops and Burberry budgie smugglers. There are Lots of footballers in Puerto banus and very expensive prostitutes, The Navy bar is full of them. £1000 a night, but all stunning girls. We were in the famous Sinatra's bar, and the Everton football team came in, they were having a weekend away together, a team bonding thing. I was there with Gary, Frank and John and we were in the company of Steve Watson who played for Everton at the time. He was good company and I ended up at the Navy bar with him. My friends had all gone home. The next thing I remember I woke up in bed with a young lady I didn't recognise, and all my money had been stolen. I think I had been drugged and taken to this complex in Andalucía. I got dressed and somehow made it out onto the street and with the little money that was left in my pocket I got a cab back to my hotel. That was a bad experience, lucky my friends had cash to help me enjoy the rest of the holiday, I borrowed a few quid and tried to forget what happened to me. That night we went to the casino that was attached to our hotel and went straight to the roulette table, my pals gave me 20 euros each and I changed the cash into chips, first bet, I put it all on red, we won!! I repeated the bet three times and each time we won. We left the casino a lot richer and decided to get a nice meal with the winnings. The Chinese meal was lovely, no expense spared, my luck was changing.

The next night we had money left over from our winnings and we went upmarket at a fantastic sea-food restaurant, this is my favourite cuisine, quality fish, I went for Lobster and picked it from a fish tank next to our table, and it was a whopper. It was the best Lobster I have ever eaten, it was succulent and clean tasting, very fresh.

23rd July 2011 I was at Lingfield racecourse for a summers evening meeting with Albert, Scooter, John, Stevie, and Gary we occasionally met up at a racecourse for a few bets and a couple of beers. It was the night we all learned that Amy Winehouse had died. It was so shocking, yet we all suspected she was on a slippery path with the drugs and the booze. I would have to say that Valerie was one of the best pop songs of all time, I have never known a reaction to a song like it. She recorded some fantastic music and I still play Valerie at most of my gigs to this day.

A man phoned me up and asked me if I could play at his son's birthday party at Brixton town hall, I took the details and turned up as requested. Parking was a nightmare, and I had to get the sound system up two flights of stairs into what looked like a conference room. I set up the gear and did a sound and light check as usual and waited for the guests to arrive. It was very clear this wasn't going to be a usual sort of gig when I saw the guests arriving. The guests were all African and dressed in traditional costume. Nigerian national dress, lots of green and the women wore head dresses that also had a lot of green in them. Then the bombshell came. They wanted me to play Nigerian music all night till 11pm and provided me with a box of vinyl 12-inch singles of African dance classics! This was going to be a long night. My twin decks never played such tripe. I wanted to end my life there and then, I had four more hours of it! But boy, did they love it, they kept on dancing all night long, following each other round the dance floor. I wanted to play a bit of Rick Astley or something, but I think I would have got lynched. At the end of the night the birthday boy came up to me and said everyone had enjoyed the music and asked if I was available in November for his younger brother's party, I had to swerve it, as it really wasn't my bag, but it was an experience I never will forget.

Jeff Witsey booked me for his 50th birthday party on board the pride of London River boat, Jeff has been a friend of mine since we were teenagers, and it was lovely he thought of me to play the music on his big night. He invited lots of people I knew and put loads of money behind the bar for his guests to drink freely all night long. It's a great venue and sails up and down the river taking in all the sights of London along the way. I did my bit, playing the music he loved and made sure all his guests had a good boogie throughout the night "American pie" and the Beatles classic "I saw her standing there" went down a treat. Well done, Jeff, for celebrating your 50th in style.

I don't think I truly realised what I did for my community during the pandemic, many have stopped me in the street and thanked me personally. Some explain to me in detail how the music and all the fun on the radio made them feel connected with their family and friends again. I listened to them, but I never really understood. Until recently, when I was doing a gig in Wrotham and my good friend Danny Heard and his wife Karen were there. It was a great wedding anniversary party at The Moat, for a couple celebrating sixty years together. During the night Danny came up to me very emotional and said to me, with emotion in his face and voice " Noel, I will never forget what you did for my mum, as long as I live" He gave me a hug, and repeated "What you did was unbelievable, and I will never forget what you did" Danny was referring to the tribute we did on Bermondsey radio for his mum, Carole, who had passed away. It suddenly hit me. How much it had meant to him. I get it now. I am so pleased I could help.

Chapter 16

BIG FINISH

Writing this book has been Therapeutic, by writing it, it has taken off a load of pressure from my shoulders and set the record straight. For the first time you will see how I got here, in my own words, rather than other people guessing, and gossiping, believe it or not even people in Bermondsey gossip. My true intention was to write this book and thank the people that helped me through the pandemic. But I thought while I was at it, I might as well start at the beginning I hope it doesn't come across as showing off or being arrogant. It's just telling my life story and the way it was.

One of my best mates questioned a section of the book! Look, this is how it was, everything in the book is true, and it makes me laugh out loud when people question it.

I said I would write 70,000 words, I that is what I have done, over 200 pages about my life and the forming of Bermondsey radio. I have done what I promised, and I hope you have enjoyed the read. It is my way of saying thank you to those that helped me. Now you have it in your hands. My book for you all. How I did it I don't know. But I did it for you all.

Firstly, I would like to thank my parents for bringing me up to respect people and treat them with kindness and humility. Everything you see in me, is a direct reflection of my mum and dad. My brother Pat, sisters Breda, Lill and Lorraine for guiding me and encouraging me throughout the years. All my great friends throughout the years, the drinking the joking, the lifetime of memories. All the Bermondsey radio team, the sponsors, the listeners, the ones that take part and the ones that donated. All those people that booked me for the most special days of their lives.

Now let us all take a breath and look back over the past 200 pages and take it all in, let's review what has just happened to a young boy from Bermondsey. Born in St Thomas hospital at 7pm on the 17th of January 1961, to John Smyth and his wife Bridget from Ireland. Shortly after he was Christened at St Georges Cathedral in Southwark, lived in 62 Campbell buildings Waterloo, before moving to 19 Rudge house on the Dickens Estate Bermondsey. Educated at St Josephs School and St Michaels secondary School. Worked at the Venus fish bar on Jamaica road and the Farmhouse kitchen. Then Christians and Co, Mobile merchandising. Guys hospital radio. 5 years on the luxury cruise ship MV La Palma, played in every single pub in Bermondsey. All the top west end hotels including the Dorchester on Park Lane. Worked at the House of commons for 20 years. Wedding DJ at venues across the world. Travelled the globe including Australia, USA, the Caribbean, and India. Seen the best recording artists on the planet. Played with global and UK music stars at the Bermondsey carnival. Formed a community radio station to help his people get through the covid 19 nightmare. And now has written a book to thank the people that helped him through the world's largest pandemic. Bermondsey boy did, ok?

Have I missed anything? Well yes quite a bit really, thousands of gigs a million great memories, hundreds of great friends, and no doubt a few enemies along the way. Wouldn't have it any other way.

If you enjoyed the book, please tell your friends, and see if we can get some Christmas presents for local children in these hard times. Thank you for being part of my life, it's been a blast, see you on the dance Floor. Noel Bermondsey's number one DJ.

BIG THANKS

Special thanks to my mum and dad, my whole family in England and Ireland. My friends, old and new. The people that booked me for their special occasions. The donators and the haters. The admin team from Bermondsey radio -my friends for life. My listeners, the ones that take part, and the many that just listen. My sponsors, every one of you. Maria for providing the pen and pad to help me over the line.

I thank you all, with all my heart, the love I have for you people is immeasurable and this book is for you. NOEL

My final thought.......

"Its nice to be important, but its much more important to be nice!"

Noel – Bermondsey's number one DJ

Printed in Great Britain
by Amazon

13685640R00119